Practical Chinese Reader 1

Patterns and Exercises

New and Revised
Traditional Character Edition

實用漢語課本

Practical Chinese Reader I
Patterns and Exercises

New and Revised
Traditional Character Edition

漢 字 作 業 簿

繁體字本

【語法結構】

【翻譯】【詞序】【用詞】【問答】【作文】

陳曼麗

Madeline Men-li Chu

Cheng & Tsui Company

About the Author

Madeline Men-li Chu is Associate Professor of Chinese language and literature at Kalamazoo College. Prior to her appointment to the endowed chair at Kalamazoo College in 1988, she taught at Oberlin College (Assistant Professor and then Asia House Director, 1978-80), Connecticut College (Assistant Professor, 1980-86), and the University of Massachusetts, Amherst (Five Colleges Associate Professor, 1986-88). While still in Taiwan, she taught at the prestigious First Girls' High School and the World College of Journalism. She has taught beginning to advanced language courses, both modern and classical, as well as literature in translation and original language literature. She has authored many articles and contributed to major works, such as the *Indian Companion to Classical Chinese Literature* and *Waiting for the Unicorn*. Madeline Chu received her B.A. degree in Chinese language and literature from National Taiwan University, and her M.A. and Ph.D degrees from the University of Arizona, Tuscon.

Cheng & Tsui Company
25 West Street
Boston, MA 02111-1268 USA
e-mail ct@world.std.com

Library of Congress Catalog Number: 90-091839

New and Revised Traditional Character Edition ISBN 0-88727-187-1
New and Revised Simplified Character Edition ISBN 0-88727-233-9

Printed in the United States of America

Companion textbook, writing workbooks, computer software, video tapes and audio tapes are available from the publisher.

PUBLISHER'S NOTE

The Cheng & Tsui Company is pleased to announce the most recent volume of the *C&T Asian Language Series,* the new and revised edition of *Practical Chinese Reader I: Patterns and Exercises.* The new and revised edition incorporates a new font style and supplements the highly successful introductory Chinese language textbook *Practical Chinese Reader I,* developed by the Beijing Language Institute.

The C&T Asian Language Series is designed to publish and widely distribute quality language texts as they are completed by teachers at leading educational institutions. *The C&T Asian Language Series* is devoted to significant works in the field of Asian languages developed in the United States and elsewhere.

We welcome readers' comments and suggestions concerning the publications in this series. Please contact the following members of the Editorial Board:

Contents

Acknowledgments

First, I would like to thank those who used the 1989, 1990 and 1992 editions of the *PCRI Patterns and Exercises.* Your interest and encouragement are greatly appreciated. This current volume contains additional new features. While it keeps the general content of the 1992 "new and expanded edition," it adds more notes for clarification and more communicative exercises. It also uses a different, and more beautiful, typesetting for the Chinese characters.

Many people have provided valuable assistance in the writing of this book during its earlier stages. The beginning of the first draft was made possible by a sub-Mellon Grant awarded by the Executive Committee of the Five Colleges Foreign Language Resource Center, Amherst, Massachusetts. I want to thank my former colleagues at the Five Colleges: Ted Yao, Grace Fong, Alvin Cohen, and Ling-hsia Yeh who used the first and second drafts of the exercises in their classes and offered me valuable comments. My special thanks go to Shou-hsin Teng of the University of Massachusetts, whose leadership and organizational ability were the soul of the entire venture. Without his encouragement this project would have been aborted at its initial point. The encouragement and suggestions of members of the editorial board of the Cheng & Tsui Publishing Company were most useful in guiding me in the revision of its first edition.

The support of Kalamazoo College for providing me with the necessary facilities and personnel assistants has made the job of subsequent revisions much easier. I also want to thank Katheryn Rajnak and Fusen Han for their help in making the computer much more friendly. For this most recent revision, my thanks go to Jane Parish Yang and Ned VanderVen for their valuable comments, to Sun Qingshun for his help with the typing, and to my students at Kalamazoo College for their continuing feedback. Of course, I am solely responsible for any remaining errors and shortcomings.

Spiritual support has always been the most important energizing force behind my work. As always, my husband, John, and my sons, Robert and Andy, have supported me in every way. They make me feel that my work is important. My family, therefore, deserves the ultimate credit for this book.

Madeline Chu
Kalamazoo College
Summer 1993

Introduction

PCR I: Patterns and Exercises is a book of sentence patterns and written exercises published as a companion volume for the textbook *Practical Chinese Reader I. The Practical Chinese Reader* series have a particular strength in introducing practical expressions and helping initiate useful conversations. However, one shortcoming of the texts is their failure to systematically introduce the basic grammatical structure of Chinese, an essential component in developing a useful understanding of the language and in establishing a solid foundation for more advanced use of the language. Supplementary materials are necessary to make these texts effective.

PCR I: Patterns and Exercises was written to meet this need. With pattern illustrations and exercises, it provides supplementary materials to assure effective use of the language elements introduced in the textbook. For a language such as Chinese that has no inflectional endings but depends heavily on syntax to express grammatical relations, pattern analysis is of ultimate importance. The pattern illustration first identifies fundamental sentence structures and then dissects the sentences and explains the function of each constituent element. The pattern illustrations provide a starting point for the accompanying exercises. The incorporated exercises would help students establish a systematic understanding of the linguistic and cultural elements introduced in the textbook and to increase their sensitivity of the general characteristics of the Chinese language.

Five types of exercises are included: (1) *Translation*, to familiarize the student with the sentence patterns associated with each lesson and offer enough opportunity for hands-on exercises by applying the patterns for making meaningful statements; (2) *Word Order*, to train the student to observe the important sequence of elements in each type of sentence and explore different possibilities of ordering these elements; (3) *Choice of Words*, to sharpen the student's sensitivity to the semantic and grammatical nuances of words and phrases, and the roles they play in different statements; (4) *Answering Questions*, to help the student review the content as well as the grammatical points of the lessons in the textbook, and to enhance their ability to communicate in the language; and (5) *Composition*, to train the student to organize their thoughts around the acquired Chinese vocabularies and sentence patterns and to connect sentences into paragraphs, so as to express themselves in Chinese actively and meaningfully.

Together, these exercises provide plenty opportunities for the students to learn to use the language in a wide range of realistic situations. They are designed to help the student in the reading and writing aspects of learning process. They encourage the student to practice writing characters with a purpose and they provide sufficient opportunity to enable him/her to become familiar with these characters. At the same time, they offer variety and eliminate monotony caused by the conventional assignment of writing the same character time and again. They would reinforce the student's understanding of the language through doing the exercises. Furthermore, because these exercises are organized according to the level of difficulty, they may be straight-forward yet interesting, challenging yet not frustrating. Three vocabulary finding lists, as well as two character finding lists, are appended for conveniently finding a character or a vocabulary item. Additionally, a simplified-regular character conversion table is attached for easy reference.

It is the author's hope that the pattern illustrations, language-use explanations, examples and exercises will reduce to a minimum the need for in-class factual exposition so that class time may be more efficiently used in the development of listening and speaking skills.

Abbreviations

Adj	Adjective
Adv	Adverb
Co-V	Co-verb
Conj	Conjunction
Exp	Expression
IM	Initiation Marker
Info	Information
MM	Manner Marker
Modif	Modifier
Neg	Negative
NP	Noun Phrase
Obj	Object
Pred	Predicate
Pron	Pronoun
Q-w	Question Word
Subj	Subject
V	Verb
V-act	Verb of Action
V-ex	Verb of Existence
V-id	Verb of Identity
V-mtn	Verb of Motion
V-st	Verb of State
VP	Verb Phrase

Exercise I
(Lessons 1-3)

A. 翻譯 Translation: Apply the illustrated pattern to translate the sentences into Chinese.

Pattern #1: **Descriptive Sentence:** Describing the state of people (or things).

	The subject		**is in this state.**
	Subj: NP	\<Neg.\>	Predicate: V-state
[Examples]:	我	不	忙.
	他們		都很好.

1. He is not busy.   他不忙

2. They are fine.   他們好

3. Both my older brother and my younger brother are very busy.

   我的哥哥和我的弟弟都很忙

4. His younger brother is also very busy.

   他的弟弟也很忙

5. His older brother and my older brother are both nice.

   他的哥哥和我的哥哥都很好

6. Gubo is fine.

   Gubo 很好

7. Palanka is busy, too.

   Palanka 也忙

8. You are not busy. They are not busy, either.

   你不忙。他們不也忙。

9. They are both quite well.

   他們都很好。

10. All of us are also not very busy.

    我們都也不很忙。

Exercise I (Cont.)

B. 翻譯 Translation : Apply the illustrated patterns to translate the sentences into Chinese.

Pattern #2:   **Interrogative Sentence**: Using Question-word 嗎 to verify a statement.

	The subject is in this state	**right**?
	Statement: sentence	Q-w 嗎
[Example]:	他 不 忙	嗎?

Pattern #3:   **Interrogative Sentence**: Using Question-word 呢 to compare situations.

	Subj. 1	**is in this state.**	**Subj. 2**	**the same**?
	Subj. 1	Pred. 1	Subj. 2	Q-w 呢?
[Example]:	我	好,	你	呢?

1. "How are you?" "I'm very well, and you?"
   你好? 我很好,你呢?

2. How is your older brother?
   他的哥哥 嗎?

3. Is neither his older brother nor his younger brother nice?
   他的哥哥和他的弟弟都不好嗎?

4. Are you busy?
   你忙嗎?

5. Are they also busy?
   他們也忙嗎?

6. I am not very busy. How about you?
   我不很忙。你呢?

7. I am fine. How about you?
   我很好。你呢?

8. His older brother is busy. How about his younger brother?
   他的哥哥忙。他的弟弟呢?

9. You are not very busy. How about him?
   你不很忙。他呢?

10. Both my older brother and younger brother are not very busy. How about your brothers?
    我哥哥和弟弟都不很忙。你的哥哥,弟弟 呢?

2

Exercise I (Cont.)

C. 詞序 Word Order: Rearrange the elements of each entry to make a grammatical sentence.

Note: Refer to the patterns listed previously and the following order of modifiers.

Subject			**Predicate**
[Subj.]		(也)	<Neg.> 都 <Neg.> 很 忙 嗎?

1. 都   他們   忙   很

   他們都很忙

   Both of them are very busy.
   Ta men dou hen mang

2. 好   很   也   他

   他也很好

   He also is very well.
   Ta ye hen hao.

3. 我   忙   呢   不   你

   我不忙,你呢?

   I am not busy, and you?
   Wo bu mang, ni ne?

4. 都   他哥哥   不忙   他弟弟

   他哥哥(and)他弟弟都不忙。

   His older bro. + his younger bro. are both not busy.
   Ta gege and ta didi dou bu mang.

5. 不   也   你   嗎   忙

   你不也忙嗎?

   You are not also busy, right?
   Ni bu ye mang, ma?

6. 嗎   好   你

   你好嗎?

   You well?
   Ni hao ma

7. 忙   很   嗎   都   他們

   他們都很忙嗎?

   They both are very busy right?
   Ta men dou hen mang ma

8. 也   忙   他哥哥   很

   他哥哥也很忙

   His older bro. also very busy.
   Ta gege ye hen mang

9. 呢   你   他們   都   好   很

   他們都很好,你呢?

   They both very well, and you?
   Ta men dou hen hao, Ni ne?

10. 都   他們   很   不   忙   也

   他們都不很忙也。

   Ta men dou bu hen mang.

Exercise I (Cont.)

D. 用詞 Choice of Words: Choose the most appropriate word or phrase from the list to complete a grammatical sentence.

1. 我很好, 你 ___呢___ ?
   (a) 嗎   (b) 呢 ⟲   (c) 也

2. 我不忙, 他們 ___也___ 不忙.
   (a) 都   (b) 很   (c) 也 ⟲

3. 他們 ___也都___ 不忙嗎?
   (a) 也都 ⟲   (b) 都很   (c) 也很

4. 你忙 ___嗎___ ?
   (a) 嗎 ⟲   (b) 呢   (c) 也

5. 他 ___不很___ 忙.
   (a) 很不   (b) 不也   (c) 不很 ⟲

6. 他們也都 ___很___ 好.
   (a) 忙   (b) 很   (c) 嗎

7. 你哥哥, 我哥哥 ___都___ 不忙.
   (a) 都 ⟲   (b) 很   (c) 也

8. ___他們___ 都忙嗎?
   (a) 你   (b) 他們 ⟲   (c) 他不

   I am very busy, you   busy right

9. 我很忙, 你 ___很___ 忙嗎?
   (a) 也很   (b) 也不   (c) 很 ⟲
   also very   also not   very

10. 他哥哥很好, 他弟弟 ___呢___ ?
    (a) 嗎   (b) 呢   (c) 也

4

Exercise I (Cont.)

E. 問答 **Questions:** Answer the following questions.

Note: Assume that in numbers 1-5 the two subjects concerned are in the same situation and that in numbers 6-10 they are not.

1. 我不忙, 你呢? 我也不忙。

2. 他們都很好, 你呢? 也很好。

3. 我好, 你呢? 也好。

4. 我很好, 你好嗎? 我很好
也

5. 他很忙, 你呢? 我也很忙。

6. 我弟弟很好, 你弟弟呢? 他也很好

7. 我不忙, 你忙嗎? 我忙

8. 我哥哥, (我)弟弟都很好. 你哥哥, (你)弟弟也都很好嗎?
我哥哥, (我)弟弟 都很好。

9. 他不好. 他哥哥好嗎?
他哥哥很好。

10. 你哥哥很忙. 你弟弟不忙嗎?
我弟弟不忙。

Exercise II
(Lessons 4-6)

A. 翻譯 Translation: Apply the illustrated pattern to translate the sentences into Chinese.

Pattern #4: **Ascriptive Sentence:** Using verb-of-identification 是 to identify the subject by profession / nationality / relation to others, etc.

	This subject		**is**	**of this identity**.
	Person(s)/Thing(s)	\<neg.>	V-id 是	ID of person(s)/thing(s)
[Examples]:	他們		是	大夫.
	這	不	是	王(Wang) 大夫.

1. He is Palanka's father.

2. They are not Chinese.

3. That is my mother's friend.

4. My older brother's friend is a doctor.

5. Are you a teacher?

6. Isn't any of them his friend?

7. This is not my younger brother's book.

8. This is his car. That is also his car.

9. Our doctor is also our friend.

10. Not all Chinese language teachers are Chinese.

Exercise II (Cont.)

B. 翻譯 Translation: Apply the illustrated pattern to translate the sentences into Chinese.

Pattern #5: Interrogative Sentences: Using question-words 誰, 誰的 or 哪國人 to inquire identity of person(s) / thing(s).

	(a) This/These person(s)	**is/are**	**of what id/nationality?**
	NP - person(s)	是	Q-word 誰 / 哪國人
[Example]	她	是	哪國人?
	(b) The person(s)/thing(s)	**is/are**	**whose relation / belonging?**
	NP - person(s)/thing(s)	是	Q-word 誰的 + NP
[Example]	這	是	誰的漢語書?
	(c) Which person(s)	**is/are**	**one(s) with this identity?**
	Q-word 誰	是	NP - person
[Example]	誰	是	大夫?
	(d) Whose relation/belonging	**is/are**	**one(s) with this identity?**
	Q-word 誰的 + NP	是	NP-person(s)/thing(s)
[Example]	誰的車	是	美(Mei3) 國車?

Note: In a Chinese sentence, an indicative noun or pronoun such as 這, 那, 他/她(們) and他/她(們)的, generally appears before the verb-id 是.

1. Who is she? 她是誰?

2. Who is a doctor? 誰是大夫

3. Which one is your Chinese language teacher?

誰是你的漢語老師 ?

4. Who is her older brother?

誰是她哥哥?

5. Whose car is this?

這是誰的車?

6. Whose car is a Japanese* car? [*=item included in the supplementary vocabulary list.]

誰的車是(Riben)車?

7. What is the nationality of your Chinese language teacher?

你的漢語老師是 那國人?

8. Who are your teacher's friends?

誰是你老師的朋友?

9. Which (of them) are Chinese and which are American*? [*=supplementary vocabulary item]

誰是中國人 誰是美國人

10. What kind of car [use "made in which country"] is her car?

她的車是 哪國車?

Exercise II (Cont.)

C. 詞序 Word Order: Rearrange the elements of each entry to make a grammatical sentence.

1. 書   是   那

    那是書

2. 爸爸   是   我   這

    這是我爸爸

3. 車   的   我   這   是

    這是我的車

4. 嗎   是   哥哥   這   她

    這是她哥哥嗎？

5. 大夫   不   是   車   的   那

    那不是大夫的車

6. 你們   她   是   朋友   的   嗎

    她朋友是你們嗎？Ta shi ne de pengyo ma.
    的

7. 是   書   弟弟   的   那   也

    那也是弟弟的書。

8. 不   我   大夫   是

    我不是大夫。

9. 誰的   老師   漢語   是   中(Zhong1)國人

    誰的漢語老師是中國人

10. 大夫   哪國   是   人   你的

    你的大夫是哪國人

Exercise II (Cont.)

D. 用詞 Choice of Words: Choose the most appropriate word or phrase from the list to complete a grammatical sentence.

1. 這 ___是___ 我媽媽.
       (a) 也　　　　　　(b) 不　　　　　　(c) 是

2. 他們 ___是___ 我朋友.
       (a) 好　　　　　　(b) 是　　　　　　(c) 不

3. 這是你 ___的___ 書嗎?
       (a) 爸爸　　　　　(b) 的　　　　　　(c) 中(Zhong1)國

4. 我爸爸, 我媽媽 _都是_ 大夫.
       (a) 都　　　　　　(b) 好　　　　　　(c) 都是

5. 她弟弟 _也是_ 我朋友.
       (a) 這是　　　　　(b) 也是　　　　　(c) 是也

6. 這 _不是_ 我媽媽的車.
       (a) 不是　　　　　(b) 都　　　　　　(c) 也

7. 我 ___的___ 車很好.
       (a) 不　　　　　　(b) 是　　　　　　(c) 的

8. 這是誰 ___的___ 書?
       (a) 呢　　　　　　(b) 的　　　　　　(c) 嗎

9. 這不是你的車, 是 _誰的_ 車?
       (a) 哪國　　　　　(b) 誰的　　　　　(c) 嗎

10. 你的朋友是 _哪國_ 人?
       (a) 哪國　　　　　(b) 誰　　　　　　(c) 誰的

Exercise II (Cont.)

E. 問答 Questions: Answer the following questions according to your real-life situation.

1. 誰是你的漢語老師？

   你是 洪

2. 你的老師是哪國人？

   Wo ter shi shi zhongguo
   我的老師是中國人。

3. 你媽媽是老師嗎？

   Wo mama bu shi lao shi

4. 你哥哥是大夫嗎？

   我哥哥是大夫。

5. 誰是老師？誰是大夫？

   她是大夫，他是老師。

6. 誰是法(Fa3 or Fa4)國人？

   我老師(Fa)國人。

7. 你老師的車是美(Mei3)國車嗎？

   Wo lao shi de che bu che de meiguo che

8. 你爸爸的車是哪國車？

   Wo baba de che de guo che

9. 誰的車是德(De2)國車？

   Wa baba de che shie de guo che

10. 你的大夫是誰？

    Wo de shi daifu. shi wo baba

10

Exercise III
(Review: Lessons 1-6)

A. 翻譯 Translation: Apply the patterns learned so far to translate the following sentences into Chinese.

1. Are all doctors very nice? Are they all very busy?

   大夫都很好嗎？他們都很忙嗎？

2. Not all doctors are very nice. Not all of them are very busy, either.

   大夫不是都很好。他們不是都很忙。

3. His mother is a doctor. She is very busy. His father is also a doctor. He is not very busy.

   他媽媽是大夫。她很忙。他爸爸也是大夫。他不很忙。

4. Neither my mother nor my father is a doctor. They are teachers.

   我媽媽，我爸爸都不是大夫。他們是老師。

5. Her mother and her father are both very busy. They are both well, too.

   她媽媽，她爸爸都很忙。他們也很好。
   都

6. This is my younger brother. That is my younger brother's friend.

   這是我弟弟。那是我弟弟的朋友。

7. My younger brother is a doctor. His friend is also a doctor.

   我弟弟是大夫。他朋友也是大夫。
   的

8. That is his car. His car is an American car.

   那是他的車。他的車是(Mei)國車。

9. His American car is very good.

   他的(Mei)國車很好。

10. My car is a Chinese car. It [use "my car"] is also very good.

    我的車是中國車。我的車也很好。

11

owner,
origin
write about
5 sentences.

Exercise III (Cont.)

B. 作文 Composition: Write a short passage describing the following picture. For example, you may refer to the two vehicles in terms of their relative position from where you stand, you may write about the size, the quality, the ownership, and their country of origin.

·1973 VW BUG·

Joe McFadden's
1966 Pontiac GTO

You are here.

Exercise III (Cont.)

C. 作文 **Composition:** write a short passage describing the following picture. For example, you may refer to the two books in terms of their relative position from where you stand, you may write about the size, the content, the quality, and the ownership of them.

You are here.

D. 作文 **Composition:** Write a short paragraph about one of your friends' family. For example you may write about his/her parents, brothers, doctors, friends. You may also add a few things about some of these people in terms of their nationalities, professions, and belongings.

在

Exercise IV
(Lessons 7-9)

A. 翻譯 Translation: Apply the illustrated pattern to translate the sentences into Chinese.

Pattern #6: **Narrative Sentence:** Using Verb-of-action to describe habit or action.

Someone		**does**	**something**.
Subj: NP-person	<neg.>	V-act	Obj.: NP

[Example]: 我朋友   不   喝   茶.

Pattern #7: **Imperative Sentence:** Using word of request 請 to make a polite request.

Please	**do**	**this**.
請	V-act	Obj.: NP

[Example]: 請   看   地圖.

Pattern #8: **Interrogative Sentence:** using idiom 請問 to make a polite inquiry.

May I ask	**this question**?
Idiom 請問	interrogative sentence

[Example]: 請問   你是大夫嗎?

1. He smokes. None of his friends smoke.

   Ta xi yen.   Ta de peng you dou bu xi yen

2. All my friends read Chinese newspapers* [*=supplementary vocabulary item].

   Wo de peng you dou kan zhongguo bao zi

3. Our Chinese language teacher doesn't drink milk*.

   Wo men de Hanyu lao shi bu he niunai

4. I'm reading a Chinese language textbook.

   Wo kan Hanyu shu.
   zai

5. Both my older brother and my younger brother study Chinese language.

   Wǒ gége, wǒ dìdi dōu xue Hanyu.

6. Please look at the map of China. [Use the character for "Zhong1" if you can.]

   qing kan zhongguo ditu

7. May I ask, who drinks tea?

   qing wen, shei he cha

8. May I ask, is this your map?

   qing wen, zhe shi ni de ditu ma?

9. Could you tell me who is Mr. Ding? [The character for Ding is 丁.]

   qing wen, shei shi ding xiesheng

10. Could you tell me what you are watching?

    qing wen, ni kan shenme?
    zai

14

Exercise IV (Cont.)

B. 翻譯 Translation: Apply the illustrated pattern to translate the sentences into Chinese.

Pattern #9: **Interrogative Sentence:** Using Question-word 甚麼 / 甚麼+ to inquire about thing(s), or kind of thing(s) or person(s).

	(a) **This**	**is**	**what <+>?**
	NP-indicative pron	V-id	Q-word 甚麼 / 甚麼 + NP
[Example]:	這	是	甚麼 / 甚麼車﹖
	(b) **What <+>**		**is / are in this state?**
	Q-word 甚麼 / 甚麼 + NP		V-state
[Example]:	甚麼 / 甚麼車		好﹖

1. What's that? [Literally: "That is what?" (See **Note** on p. 7.)]

   那是什麼?

2. What kind of map is that? [Literally: "That is what map?"]

   那是什麼地圖?

3. What kind of pen/pencil* is this [*=supplementary vocabulary item]?

   那是什麼筆?

4. What kind of car does your friend have? [Literally: "Your friend's car is what car?"]

   你朋友的車是什麼車?

5. May I ask, what would you like to drink? [= ...what do you drink?]

   請問那, na shi shenme?

6. Could you tell me [= May I ask] what books are good?

   請問那是什麼書好?

7. May I ask, what are you studying?

   請,你在學習什麼?

8. Who is that? [Use "What person...."]

   那是誰?

9. Could you tell me what is "pi2jiu3"*?

   請問,啤酒是什麼?

10. Who is greeting [= welcoming] her?

   誰歡迎她?
   在

Exercise IV (Cont.)

C. 翻譯 **Translation**: Apply the illustrated pattern to translate the sentences into Chinese.

Pattern #10: Ascriptive Sentence: Using Verb-of-identification 姓 or 叫 to identity the subject by name.

The subject		is named	so-and-so.
NP-person	\<neg.\>	V-id 姓	NP-family name
NP-person	\<neg.\>	V-id 叫	NP-given/full name
NP-thing	\<neg.\>	V-id 叫	NP-name

[Examples]: 我的老師　　　　他　　姓　　　　王 (Wang2).

他　　不　　叫　　王大好.

Note: Family name precedes one's title of addressing; for example: 謝大夫.

1. May I ask, whose family name is Wang?

　請問, 他姓王嗎?　　　　誰姓王嗎?

2. Our doctor's family name is Wang and his given name is Zhong1shu1.

　我們的大夫姓王, 他叫中書。

3. My friend's younger brother is named Ding1 Da4zhong1.

　我的朋友弟弟 叫丁大中。

4. He is an American*. His last name is Johnson and his first name is Don.

　他是美國. 他姓 Johnson, 他叫 Don.

5. My friend's Chinese car is nicknamed "Shanghai* Doctor." [*=supplementary vocabulary item]

　我的朋友的中國車叫上海大夫。

6. Is your Chinese friend's family name Che? [Do you know the character for che1?]

　你的中國朋友姓車嗎?

7. Dr. Ding's older brother's name is Da4you3.

　丁大夫哥哥叫大友。

8. Mr. Che, the teacher [=Che1 Lao3shi1] is very busy.

　車老師很忙。

9. Mrs.* Xie4's mother's maiden name is Huang2 (黃) and her full name is Huang2 Da4mei3 (美).

　謝太太媽媽姓黃, 她叫黃大美。

10. Both Dr. Xie and Dr. Che have the given name Mei3fu1.

　謝大夫, 車大夫都 → 叫美夫。

Exercise IV (Cont.)

D. 詞序 Word Order: Rearrange the elements of each entry to make a grammatical sentence.

1. 都   我們   煙   不   吸

   我們都不吸煙。

2. 甚麼   是   那

   那是甚麼。

3. 這   地圖   是   的   誰

   這是誰的地圖

4. 茶   請   喝

   請喝茶。

5. 她   丁雲 (Ding Yun)   丁 (Ding)   姓   叫

   她姓丁,她叫丁雲。

6. 您   姓   貴   請   問

   請問,您貴姓?

7. 哪國   是   她   留學生

   她是哪國留學生。

8. 甚麼   地圖   你   看

   你看甚地。

9. 也   老師   你們   的   車   姓   嗎

   你們的老師也姓車嗎?

10. 叫   朋友   的   他   大生   不

   他的朋友不叫大生。

Exercise IV (Cont.)

E. 用詞 Choice of Words: Choose the most appropriate word or phrase from the list to complete a grammatical sentence.

1. 這是 _____ 地圖？
       (a) 哪   (b) 誰   (c) 甚麼

2. _____ 是大夫？
       (a) 哪   (b) 誰   (c) 甚麼

3. 他是 _____ 人？
       (a) 哪   (b) 誰   (c) 甚麼

4. 那是 _____ 的書？
       (a) 我   (b) 誰   (c) 甚麼

5. 這不是你的車，是 _____ 車？
       (a) 哪國   (b) 誰的   (c) 甚麼

6. _____ 漢語老師不是中(Zhong1)國人？
       (a) 哪國   (b) 誰的   (c) 甚麼

7. 美(Mei3)國筆(bi3)不好，_____ 筆好？
       (a) 哪國   (b) 誰的   (c) 甚麼

8. 這不是漢語書，是 _____ 書？
       (a) 哪國   (b) 誰的   (c) 甚麼

9. 那不是中國地圖，是 _____ 地圖？
       (a) 哪國   (b) 誰的   (c) 甚麼

10. 你哥哥的好朋友是 _____ ？
       (a) 哪   (b) 誰   (c) 甚麼

Exercise IV (Cont.)

F. 用詞 Choice of Words: Choose the most appropriate word or phrase from the list to complete a grammatical sentence.

1. _____ ,你們都吸煙嗎?
    (a) 請   (b) 請問   (c) 請你

2. 他不 _____ 茶.
    (a) 是   (b) 好   (c) 喝

3. "那是 _____ 車?" "那是日本(Ri4ben3)* 車." [*=supplementary word]
    (a) 誰的   (b) 哪國   (c) 甚麼

4. 古波(Gubo) _____ 朋友叫帕蘭卡(Palanka).
    (a) 是   (b) 好   (c) 的

5. 她的弟弟 _____ 謝漢夫.
    (a) 姓   (b) 叫   (c) 是不

6. 我們都 _____ 漢語.
    (a) 學習   (b) 是   (c) 好

7. 請問, 您 _____ 姓?
    (a) 甚麼   (b) 貴   (c) 謝

8. 你們的大夫不 _____ 謝嗎?
    (a) 是   (b) 叫   (c) 姓

9. _____ 不學習漢語, 他媽媽學習漢語.
    (a) 老師謝   (b) 謝大夫   (c) 大夫謝

10. "你看 _____ 書?" "我看漢語書."
    (a) 哪國   (b) 甚麼   (c) 誰的

Exercise IV (Cont.)

G. 問答 Questions:

Note: Answer questions 1-4 according to the picture of Exercise III-B.

1. 這是甚麼?

　　這是車。

2. 這是誰的車?

　　這是我的車,這是我的朋友的車。

3. 這是哪國車?

　　這這是的車都是美國車。

4. 那也是美(Mei3)國車嗎?

　　是,那也是美國車。

5. 你喝茶嗎? 你漢語老師呢?

　　我喝茶。我漢語老師

6. 請問, 誰吸煙?

　　她吸煙。

7. 你爸爸媽媽都吸煙嗎?

　　我爸爸媽媽不都吸煙。

　　May I ask, Ding Yun is what college's student

8. 請問, 丁雲(Ding Yun)是甚麼學院的學生?

　　她漢語學院的學生。

9. 她學習甚麼?

　　她學習漢言。

　　Ta kan bao ma

10. 她看報(bao4)嗎?

Exercise V
(Lessons 10-12)

A. 翻譯 Translation: Apply the illustrated pattern to translate the sentences into Chinese.

Pattern #11: Ascriptive Sentence: Using Verb-of-existence 在 / 住 / 住在 to indicate location of the subject.

The subject		lives at / is at	this place.
NP	<neg.>	V-ex 在 / 住 / 住在	NP - place
[Example]: 謝老師	不	住在	宿舍.

Pattern #12: Interrogative Sentence: Using Q-word 嗎 or 哪兒 to inquire about location of the subject.

(a) Someone/something	is at this place	right?
Sentence of Location		Q-word 嗎
[Example]: 丁雲(Ding Yun)	在宿舍	嗎?

(b) Subject	lives at / is at	where?
NP - person/thing	V-exist 在 / 住 / 住在	Q-word 哪兒
[Example]: 她弟弟	在	哪兒?

1. Is Ms. Ding, the teacher [= Ding1 Lao3shi1] in?

丁老師在嗎?

2. She is not in.

她不在。

3. Not all foreign students live in the dormitory.

留學生不都住宿舍。

4. May I ask, where does your older brother live? Does he live in China?

請問, 你哥哥住哪兒? 他住中國?

5. He does not live in China. He lives in France.

他不住中國。他住法國。
　　在　　　　　在

6. We both live on the third floor. He lives in No. 345; I live in No. 301.

我們都住四層。他住在 三四五, 我住在 三〇一。

7. Isn't Dr. Xie at the hospital*?

謝大夫在 hospital 嗎

8. Her mother is in the hospital*. [*=supplementary word]

她媽媽在 hospital。

9. Could you tell me where is his English dictionary?

請問他美國詞典哪兒?

英語

10. His English dictionary is not here*. His English pictorial is here*.

他美國詞典不住在。

Ying yu.

21

Exercise V (Cont.)

B. 翻譯 Translation: Apply the illustrated pattern to translate the sentences into Chinese.

Pattern # 13: Position of Time-word

	(a) **Subject**	**at this time**	**<neg.>**	**is in this state.**
	NP	Time-word		Predicate
[Example]:	謝老師	現在		在宿舍.
	(b) **At this time**	**the subject**	**<neg.>**	**is in this state.**
	Time-word	NP		Predicate
[Example]:	現在	他弟弟	不	學習英語.

1. Where is he now?

2. Thank you. I don't want to drink [use "I don't drink"] tea right now.

3. He is not a teacher. He is a student now.

4. Her older brother is currently studying Chinese.

5. The doctor is very busy at this moment.

6. These days, are you using the Chinese dictionary often?

7. Who lives in No. 514 these days?

8. The exchange students are now studying in our dormitory.

9. Do you use the world* atlas* now? [*=supplementary word. Also, you may use the same Chinese word for "map" and "atlas."]

10. Now he often goes to see his girl friend.

Exercise V (Cont.)

C. 翻譯 Translation: Apply the illustrated pattern to translate the sentences into Chinese.

Pattern #14: Narrative Sentence: Using verb-of-motion, place word, and verb-of-action to describe motion, destination and purpose.

Someone		**comes /goes to**	**this place**	**to do this.**
NP - person	<neg>	V-motion	NP -place	V-act+Obj:NP
[Example]: 他		去	宿舍	看 朋友.

1. He goes to the Foreign Language Institute to study French.

2. His girlfriend does not go to his dormitory to see him.

3. Where should we go to have some tea? [= Where do we go...?]

4. Is your younger brother going to China to study Chinese?

5. I often go to my friend's dorm to use his Chinese dictionary.

6. Her father often goes to the hospital* to see the doctor. [*=supplementary word]

7. She is now going to the Medical College [=yi1xue2yuan4] to return the books.

8. She is now going to Room 698 to see a friend.

9. Who's going to the Foreign Language Institute to welcome the exchange students?

10. Are you all going to Ding Yun's dormitory to thank her?

Exercise V (Cont.)

D. 詞序 Word Order: Rearrange the elements in each entry to make a grammatical sentence.

1. 我   不   詞典   用   現在

2. 丁雲 (Ding Yun)   畫報   他   還

3. 你   我   宿舍   住   呢

4. 朋友   的   帕蘭卡 (Palanka)   不   畫報   看

5. 學生   外語學院   的   都   這兒   在

6. 漢語   老師   認識   誰   他們的

7. 他們   我的   朋友   好   是   都   也

8. 他   書   哪兒   還   去

9. 你   呢   喝茶   現在   去   我們

10. 漢語   女朋友   車大夫的 學習   去   中 (Zhong1)國

Exercise V (Cont.)

E. 用詞 **Choice of Words**: Choose the most appropriate word or phrase from the list to complete a grammatical sentence.

1. 請問, 廁所(ce4suo3)* _____ 哪兒? [*=supplementary word]
      (a) 去   (b) 在   (c) 是

2. 你現在 _____ 畫報嗎?
      (a) 甚麼   (b) 用   (c) 看

3. 我們常去外語學院 _____.
      (a) 朋友   (b) 學習   (c) 英語

4. 古波(Gubo) _____ 醫院(yi1yuan4)* 看大夫.
      (a) 朋友   (b) 現在   (c) 去

5. 我認識古波, 我也 _____ 帕蘭卡(Palanka).
      (a) 認識   (b) 朋友   (c) 看

6. 他 _____ 不喝茶.
      (a) 現在   (b) 去   (c) 宿舍

7. 您去 _____ 看朋友?
      (a) 現在   (b) 哪兒   (c) 甚麼

8. 他們都是 _____ 大夫.
      (a) 很好   (b) 很好的   (c) 認識

9. _____ 我們去宿舍看她.
      (a) 現在   (b) 學生   (c) 誰

10. _____ 看畫報.
      (a) 不   (b) 請   (c) 甚麼

Exercise V (Cont.)

F. 問答 Questions: Answer the following questions according to facts of your real life and the information provided in the lessons.

1. 外語學院的學生都住宿舍嗎？老師呢？

2. 你住在宿舍嗎？你住多少號？你朋友住哪兒？

3. 誰是古波(Gubo) 的女朋友？她是哪國人？

4. 他們都學習漢語嗎？

5. 他們常用漢語詞典嗎？你呢？

6. 他們的老師是哪國人？他姓甚麼？

7. 他是很好的漢語老師嗎？

8. 丁雲(Ding Yun) 是誰？她認識帕蘭卡(Palanka) 嗎？

9. 丁雲也學習漢語嗎？[You may also try to answer this question: 英語呢？]

10. 帕蘭卡常去哪兒看丁雲？

Exercise VI
(Review: Lessons 7-12)

A· 用詞 **Choice of Words**: Fill in each blank with an appropriate Chinese character to make each entry a grammatical sentence.

Note: It is possible that there are more than one correct answers.

1. 誰 _____ (_____) 六二五號?

2. _____ _____ 她不 _____ 報. [Hint: What may appear before the subject?]

3. 還 _____ 報紙(zhi3)*, 謝謝. [*=supplementary word]

4. 古波(Gubo) _____ 女朋友住 _____ _____ ?

5. " _____ 坐, _____ 喝茶." "謝謝您." " _____ _____ _____."

6. 請問, 謝先生 _____ 嗎?

7. 請 _____, 法語詞典 _____ 哪兒?

8. 她還你 _____ _____ ?

9. _____ 還他畫報?

10. 我們老師不 _____ 謝. 他 _____ 不 _____ 法國人.

Exercise VI (Cont.)

B. 作文 Composition: (Part 1)

Write a passage about a series of things you plan to do, using the word 看 in each sentence. As you know, the word 看 may be used for the meaning of "looking at," "visiting (someone)," "reading" (a newspaper, magazine/ pictorial, or a book), etc.

C. 作文 Composition (Part 2):

Are you curious about something? Ask questions and find out information about them. Write a series of questions you may ask to find out information about two or three different things. Of course, interrogative words such as 甚麼, 誰, 誰的, 哪兒, 嗎, 呢, etc. are useful here.

Exercise VI (Cont.)

D. 作文 Composition (Part 3):

Write a dialogue between you and a friend who came to your place to visit. For example, you might start by greeting her at the door, asking her to come in and offering her something to drink. Later you might be discussing your study and the well being of your family members.

E. 用詞 Choice of Words: Write down the appropriate expression for each of the following occasions.

1. You are a polite person and you want to ask a question. What do you say before actually stating our question.

2. What do you say to indicate your gratitude?

3. When someone shows her gratitude to you, what do you say?

Exercise VII
(Lesson 13)

A. 翻譯 Translation: Apply the illustrated pattern to translate the sentences into Chinese.

Pattern #15: **Interrogative Sentence**: Using "V + Neg. V" structure to form a question.

Subject	Predicate				
NP	V_a-state	+	Neg. V_a		
NP	V_b-id	+	Neg. V_b	+	NP
NP	V_c-act	+	Neg. V_c	+	Object
NP	V_d-motion	+	Neg. V_d	+	NP-place

[Example]:

您	忙	不忙？	
你朋友	姓	不姓	謝？
他	吸	不吸	煙？
他們	去	不去	外語學院？

1. Is Dr. Xie busy?

2. Are you going to the store?

3. Is his girl friend's name Gu Lanlan? [Do you know how to write the characters for Gu Lanlan?]

4. Is her map of China (a) good (one)?

5. Are you studying Chinese?

6. Is her older brother a student?

7. Are you buying any paper? (Are you) buying any pens/pencils?

8. Is her boyfriend coming?

9. Does he speak Chinese?

10 Are you going to the dormitory to see Mr. Ding, the teacher [= Ding1 Lao3shi1] ?

Exercise VII (Cont.)

B. 詞序 Word Order: Rearrange the elements in each entry to make a grammatical sentence.

1. 你　　　王(Wang2)老師　　　認識　　　不認識

2. 你　　　紙　　　不買　　　買　　　請問

3. 她　　　他的　　　是　　　朋友　　　女　　　不是

4. 商店　　筆　　　去　　　買　　　誰

5. 甚麼　　弟弟　　名字　　她　　　叫

6. 古波(Gubo)　　學　　漢語　　都　　和　　帕蘭卡(Panlanka)

7. 詞典　　英語　　用　　她　　不　　常

8. 介紹　　我　　來　　一下兒

9. 哪兒　　你　　去　　喂

10. 嗎　　他們　　謝英　　不　　認識　　都

Exercise VII (Cont.)

C. 用詞 Choice of Words: Fill in the blanks with appropriate words, using one character for each blank.

Note: Review the "V + Neg. V" are other interrogative sentence patters. Also review the new words of this lesson. Remember that each exercise is meant to help you review patterns vocabulary already studied.

1. 您認識 _____ _____ _____ 車大夫？

2. 她弟弟說 _____ _____ 漢語？

3. 丁雲 (Ding Yun) _____ 朋友 _____ 不在宿舍？

4. 你們 _____ 不學習法語嗎？

5. 他們 _____ _____ 不歡迎我？

6. 你們 _____ _____ _____ 商店？ (Are you going to the store?)

7. "他爸爸來 _____ _____ ？" "他來."

8. "你們買 _____ _____ ？" "我們買筆 _____ 紙."

9. 她男朋友 _____ 英國人嗎？

10. 他姓 _____ _____ ？ (他) 叫甚麼 _____ _____ ？

32

Exercise VII (Cont.)

D. 問答 Questions: Answer the following questions according to the information provided in the lesson and your own real-life situation.

1. 帕蘭卡(Palanka) 的男朋友叫甚麼名字？

2. 古波(Gubo) 是不是中(Zhong1)國人？

3. 古波和帕蘭卡去哪兒？

4. 他們去那兒*買甚麼？丁雲(Ding Yun) 呢？ [*=supplementary word]

5. 誰學習漢語？

6. 丁雲是不是學生？

7. 她學不學英語？

8. 她認識不認識古波？

9. 你常說漢語嗎？你用不用漢語詞典？

10. 你看不看報？你看不看法語報？

Exercise VIII
(Lessons 14)

A. 翻譯 Translation: Apply the illustrated pattern to translate the sentences into Chinese.

Pattern # 16: **Ascriptive Sentence**: Using Verb-of-possession/existence 有 and its negative form 沒有 to indicate possession or existence, or the negation of such.

Someone/ some place	(does not)	have	this.
NP - person/place	<Neg.沒>	有	NP
[Example]: 帕蘭卡 (Palanka)		有	漢語詞典.
銀行 (現在)	沒	有	人.

1. We all have a Chinese dictionary.

2. Does Ding Yun have a boyfriend? [Use 嗎.]

3. Does your French language teacher have a spouse? [Use 嗎.]

4. They don't have any children.

5. The company's* manager has a car. His wife also has a car. [*=supplementary word]

6. The bookstore does not have Chinese newspapers.

7. Her child has no friends.

8. Neither of us has older sisters.

9. There are not any good doctors in the hospital*.

10. There are no exchange students in the Foreign Language Institute.

34

Exercise VIII (Cont.)

B. 翻譯 Translation: Apply the illustrated pattern to translate the sentences into Chinese.

<u>**Pattern # 17**</u>: **Interrogative Sentence**: Using 有没有 to inquire about possession or existence.

	This person / This place	**has / does not have**	**this.**
	NP - person/place	V + Neg. V 有没有	NP
[Examples]:	您	有没有	筆?
	宿舍	有没有	人?

1. Does she have a husband?

2. Do they have any children?

3. Are there any female doctors in the hospital*?

4. Do you have any sisters or brothers?

5. Are there any male employees* in the bank?

6. Does the college/university have a bookstore?

7. Are there foreign books in the bookstore?

8. Do they have a good French dictionary?

9. Does your friend have a family?

10. Does Dr. Gu have a younger sister?

Exercise VIII (Cont.)

C. 翻譯 **Translation:** Apply the illustrated pattern to translate the sentences into Chinese.

Pattern # 18: **Narrative Sentence:** Using <u>Co-verb 在 + V-of-action (+obj.)</u> to inform the location of an event.

	Someone	**at**	**this place**	**does this.**
	NP - person	Co-verb 在	NP - place	V-act (+Obj:NP)
[Example]:	我姐姐	在	宿舍	看　書

1. He is reading a newspaper in the Foreign Language Institute.

2. Where do you buy pens/pencils?

3. She works at home.

4. My brother and his girlfriend both work in the bookstore.

5. Who works at the bank?

6. Ding Yun is buying a map at the bookstore.

7. What is her younger sister buying at the store?

8. She is at home writing letters.

9. Where do his children go to school [= study]?

10. What kind of work do you do at the post office*?

Exercise VIII (Cont.)

D. 翻譯 Translation: Apply the illustrated pattern to translate the sentences into Chinese.

Pattern # 19: **Narrative Sentence**: Using the Co-verb 給 to indicate "favor" or "offering."

	Someone	for / to someone else	does	something.
	NP-person	Co-verb 給 + NP-person	V-act +	Obj.: NP
[Example]:	我	給　　我姐姐	寫	信.

Note: 給 may also be used to mean "on behalf of," "for the sake of," and "for the benefit of."

Pattern #20: **Narrative Sentence**: Using the Verb-of-action 說 or 告訴 to reiterate a statement.

	Someone	state / relates to someone else	this information.
	NP-person	V-act 說 / 告訴 + NP-person	Statement
	她	說	她去買書.
	謝友學	告訴　　我	車大夫很忙.

1. I am writing to my family.

2. Dr. Xie bought us the newspaper.

3. Her boy friend is returning the book for her.

4. Mr. Che, the teacher, [= Che1 Lao3shi1] introduced us to each other.

5. She told me she is homesick.

6. He says that you (plural) are good friends.

7. My older brother tells us that she misses home very much.

8. I told him I work for a bank.

9. He asked me where the bank is.

10. His mother is buying a pen for him.

Exercise VIII (Cont.)

E. 詞序 Word Order: Rearrange the elements in each entry to make a grammatical sentence.

1. 他　　孩子　　　沒有

2. 在　　書店　　　他愛人　　不　　　　工作

3. 妹妹　謝大夫　　沒有　　　有

4. 我　　寫信　　　給　　　常　　　　請(你)

5. 銀行　女朋友　　她　　　是　　　經理(jing1li3)*　　的

6. 他　　他　　　　說　　　工作　　郵局(you2ju2)*　　在

7. 告訴　我　　　　我　　　他　　　喝茶　　不

8. 我　　我朋友　　寫信　　給　　　常

9. 你　　他們　　　請　　　問　　　好

10. 姐姐　有　　　　沒有　　你

Exercise VIII (Cont.)

F. 用詞 Choice of Words: Fill in each blank with an appropriate character to make grammatical sentences.

1. 他 _____ 甚麼工作? (What does he do?)

2. 留學生都很 _____ 家. (... homesick.)

3. 他姐姐在 _____ _____ 工作?

4. 我常 _____ 我朋友 _____ 信.

5. 您有 _____ _____ 妹妹?

6. 他 _____ _____ 我他 _____ 想他媽媽.

7. 她 _____ 我書店有 _____ _____ 法語書. (She asks me if there is....)

8. 請 _____ 您爸爸媽媽好.

9. 她愛人不 _____ 外語學院 _____ _____ 英語.

10. 他 _____ 他哥哥常買書 _____ 他.

Exercise VIII (Cont.)

G. 問答 Questions: Answer the questions according to the information provided in the lessons.

1. 丁雲 (Ding Yun) 想不想家？想不想她爸爸媽媽？

2. 她也想她男朋友嗎？

3. 丁雲有沒有姐姐妹妹？她有沒有哥哥弟弟？

4. 她姐姐在哪兒工作？

5. 丁雲的姐姐有沒有孩子？

6. 誰在醫院(yi1yuan4)* 工作？

7. 他作甚麼工作？

8. 丁雲常給她姐姐寫信嗎？

9. 你想丁雲也常給她爸爸媽媽,她男朋友寫信嗎？

10. 丁雲在哪兒學習？她學習甚麼？

Exercise IX
(Lessons 15)

A. 翻譯 Translation: Apply the illustrated pattern to translate the sentences into Chinese.

Pattern #21: **Expression of Quantity**: <Number> + <Measure Word>

	... this many	**units of**	**people / things ...**
	Adj. - Number	Measure-word	NP - person/thing
[Examples]:	三	本	書
	六	個	學生

Pattern #22: **Interrogative Sentence**: Using Question-word 幾/多少 to inquire about quantity.

	.. how much / how many	**units of**	**people / thing ...**
	Q-word 幾	Measure-word	NP - person/thing
	Q-word 多少	(Measure-word)	NP - person/thing
[Examples]:	幾	本	雜誌
	多少	(個)	老師

1. Mr. Wang, the teacher [= Wang2 Lao3shi1] has one older brother and one younger sister.

2. The Foreign Language Institute has five teachers and forty-eight students.

3. He now knows ninety-four Chinese characters.   4. She has three Chinese friends.

5. I'll buy one world atlas and three magazines.   6. The library has three reading rooms.

7. How many departments are there in the Foreign Language Institute?

8. May I ask, how many students are there in the Chinese Department?

9. How many English and French language teachers do you have?

10. How many Chinese language grammar books are you buying?

41

Exercise IX (Cont.)

B. 翻譯 Translation: Apply the illustrated pattern to translate the sentences into Chinese.

Pattern #23: **Types of modifiers**

Modifier		Key-word/phrase/clause	
Noun - word/phrase/clause	(英國)	Noun	(人)
Adj. - word/phrase/clause	(新)	Noun	(車)
Adv. - word/phrase/clause	(很)	Adj.	(好)
Adv. - word/phrase/clause	(常)	Verb	(買)
Adv. - word/phrase/clause	(都)	Adv.	(很)...
Adv. - word/phrase/clause	(常)	Clause	(在閱覽室看書)

1. This is a <u>new</u> book.

2. I <u>often</u> buy <u>Chinese</u> magazines.

3. Are <u>new</u> cars <u>all</u> <u>very</u> <u>good</u>?

4. They <u>both</u> have <u>girl</u> friends.

5. We learn <u>from each other</u> [= mutually].

6. He does <u>not often</u> write to his mother.

7. <u>New</u> <u>American</u> cars are <u>not</u> <u>all</u> good.

8. I <u>often</u> drink <u>English</u> tea at the <u>new</u> shop.

9. He often buys French newspapers at the Student Bookstore.

10. Gubo is a <u>very good</u> friend of his. Palanka is <u>also</u> a <u>good</u> friend <u>of his</u>.

Exercise IX (Cont.)

C. 翻譯 Translation: Apply the illustrated pattern to translate the sentences into Chinese.

Pattern #24: **Compound Sentence**: Using Parallel Clauses to present similar situations.

	A	does this,	B	also	does this.
	Subj. 1	Pred.	Subj. 2	也	Pred.
	NP1	V + Obj.	NP2	也	V + Obj.
[Example]:	他	學習漢語,	他哥哥	也	學習漢語.

	A	does this,	A	also	does that.
	Subj. 1	Pred.	Subj. 2	也	Pred.
	NP1	V + Obj.	NP2	也	V + Obj.
[Example]:	他	看雜誌,	他	也	看報.

1. He doesn't drink tea. I don't, either.   2. He teaches Chinese. He also studies French.

3. Mr. Xie teaches them characters. He also teaches grammar.

4. She often writes to me. She also often writes to my younger brother.

5. They don't often buy magazines. They also don't buy newspapers.

6. There are often students in the new reading room. The old [=lao3] reading room often has students, too.

7. She often buys books for him. She also teaches him new Chinese characters.

8. The Chinese Department has five exchange students. So does the French Department.

9. He went to the library to read magazines and also to borrow* some books.

10. I have three dictionaries. I also have twenty-five Chinese books.

Exercise IX (Cont.)

D. 詞序 Word Order: Rearrange the elements in each entry to make a grammatical sentence.

1. 學生　　中文系　　九十七　　有　　　　個

2. 我們　　系　　　老師　　十　　　個　　　有

3. 我們　　學習　　互相

4. 口語　　我們　　教　　　謝老師

5. 你們　　誰　　　語法　　教

6. 雜誌　　法文　　沒有　　閱覽室

7. 我　　我　　　中文　　法文　　學習　　學習　　也

8. 幾個　　外國　　朋友　　有　　　你

9. 我　　他　　　看　　　畫報　　和　　　都

10. 幾　　詞典　　漢語　　本　　　圖書館　　有

Exercise IX (Cont.)

E. 用詞 Choice of Words: Choose the most appropriate word or phrase from the list.

1. 外語學院 _____ 多少學生?
    (a) 是　　　　　　　(b) 在　　　　　　　(c) 有

2. 王(Wang) 老師有一 _____ 女孩子.
    (a) 個　　　　　　　(b) 本　　　　　　　(c) 沒

3. 新閱覽室有六 _____ 漢語詞典.
    (a) 個　　　　　　　(b) 本　　　　　　　(c) (leave it blank)

4. 古波(Gubo)學習漢語, 帕蘭卡(Palanka) _____ 學習漢語.
    (a) 還　　　　　　　(b) 和　　　　　　　(c) 也

5. 謝大夫看報, 他 _____ 寫信.
    (a) 也　　　　　　　(b) 和　　　　　　　(c) 常

6. 她教我們漢字, _____ 我們語法.
    (a) 也她教　　　　　(b) 和她教　　　　　(c) 她也教

7. 書店有中文報 _____ 中文雜誌.
    (a) 也　　　　　　　(b) 和　　　　　　　(c) 有也

8. 她去書店買筆, 買紙, _____ 報.
    (a) 也　　　　　　　(b) 和　　　　　　　(c) 也買

9. 請問, 您有 _____ 語法書?
    (a) 三本　　　　　　(b) 多少個　　　　　(c) 幾本

10. 中文系有 _____ 留學生?
    (a) 幾　　　　　　　(b) 多少　　　　　　(c) 十二

Exercise IX (Cont.)

F. 問答 Questions: Answer the following questions according to your real-life situations.

1. 請問,你們中文系有多少學生?

2. 中文系有沒有中國老師?

3. 誰教你們語法? 漢字呢?

4. 請問,哪兒有中文畫報?

5. 那兒也有中文雜誌嗎?

6. 外語學院的閱覽室有多少法文書? 法文畫報呢?

7. 你有沒有哥哥弟弟姐姐妹妹? 有幾個?

8. 你和誰去書店?

9. 你們去買甚麼?

10. 你們圖書館有甚麼書?

Exercise X
(Lesson 16)

A. 翻譯 **Translation**: Apply the illustrated pattern to translate the sentences into Chinese.

Pattern #25: **Ascriptive Sentence: Using 的 to indicate ownership, condition, or color.**

	<u>This person/thing</u>	<u>is</u>	<u>of this kind (person/thing)</u>
	Modifier + N	V-id + (的) +	(N)
[Examples]:	這條裙子	是 新的	(裙子).
	那個車	是 她的/紅的	(車).

<u>Note</u>: This type of sentence is used to <u>describe</u> the condition or other qualities such as color and ownership of the subject. It is also useful for making comparison and contrast when parallel clauses are used. Now, compare it with the following sentences of slightly different structures:

        (a)   "這是一條新裙子."   (To identify the subject.)

        (b)   "這條裙子很新."   (To comment on the subject.)

<u>Also Note</u>: In the predicate, the noun after 的 is generally omitted.

1. This skirt is not a new one.

2. This is his shirt; this shirt is his.

2. Both her skirt and her shirt are new.

4. My shirt is white and his is blue.

5. This green skirt is my older sister's, not my younger sister's.

6. This shirt is new. That one is old.

7. This new skirt is hers. That old one is also hers.

8. Is this green skirt yours? It is very pretty [=hao3kan4].

9. "Whose jacket* is this? Is it yours?" "This one is not mine. That one is." [Reminder: *=supplementary word]

10. Mine is not new. His is not new, either.

47

Exercise X (Cont.)

B. 翻譯 Translation: Apply the illustrated pattern to translate the sentences into Chinese.

Pattern #26: **Narrative Sentence**: Using <Co-verb 從> ... <V-motion 來/去 >... <V-action> structure to describe movement, destination and purpose.

	Someone	**from**	**place 1**	**comes to / goes to**	**place 2**	**to do this**.
	NP-person	Co-V從	NP-place	來 / 去	NP-place	V-act + Obj.
[Example]:	他們	從	宿舍	去	圖書館	還　書.

1. He is going from his house to the theatre*.

2. He is going to the theatre* to buy tickets.

3. He goes from his house to the bookstore to buy (some) books for his parents.

4. I am going to the store to buy two shirts and one skirt for my younger sister.

5. They are coming to my dormitory to see my new shirts.

6. They are going from here to the Chinese (materials) reading room.

7. Her boyfriend is coming to her house from France this evening.

8. My friend and I are going there to look for that magazine now.

9. [This] evening, we are going to the Chinese Language Institute to see a Beijing Opera.

10. Who is going there to look for him?

48

Exercise X (Cont.)

C. 詞序 **Word order:** Rearrange the elements of each entry to make a grammatical sentence.

1. 京劇　　看　　　　去　　　　丁教授

2. 我們　　他　　　票　　　京劇　　兩張　　給

3. 我們　　我們家　去　　　從　　　劇場*　京劇　　看

4. 宿舍　　圖書館　去　　　從　　　他們　　還　　書

5. 甚麼　　您　　　找　　　那兒　　去

6. 我的　　是　　　裙子　　這　　　條

7. 新　　　件　　　襯衫　　是　　　那　　　的

8. 她　　　新　　　的　　　穿　　　裙子　　綠

9. 大衣　　太　　　大　　　這　　　件

10. 我們　　看　　　京劇　　晚上　　去

Exercise X (Cont.)

D. 用詞 Choice of Words: Fill in the blanks with the most appropriate words, using one character for each blank.

1. 這 ＿＿＿ 襯衫不是我 ＿＿＿. ＿＿＿ 不是新的.

2. 那 ＿＿＿ 新 ＿＿＿ 白裙子是她姐姐 ＿＿＿.

3. 我晚上 ＿＿＿ 這兒 ＿＿＿ 你家看你.

4. 我不 ＿＿＿ (wear) 這 ＿＿＿ 新大衣*, 我 ＿＿＿ 那 ＿＿＿ 舊 ＿＿＿.

5. 他們常常 ＿＿＿ 宿舍 ＿＿＿ 書店 ＿＿＿ 雜誌.

6. 他們從 ＿＿＿ ＿＿＿ 去劇場* ＿＿＿ 京劇.

7. 我有兩 ＿＿＿ 票. 我們 ＿＿＿ 看京劇.

8. 他常常從他朋友 ＿＿＿ 兒來我們 ＿＿＿ 兒找丁雲.

9. 那 ＿＿＿ 綠襯衫太大, 不好, 我不 ＿＿＿.

10. 那 ＿＿＿ 書店很大, 我們常常去 ＿＿＿ ＿＿＿ 買書.

Exercise X (Cont.)

E. 復習 **Review: Numbers and Measure Words:** Fill in the blanks using the given quantity and proper measure words.

1. _____ _____ 票 (3)   11. _____ _____ 詞典 (2)

2. _____ _____ 學生 (15)   12. _____ _____ 地圖 (10)

3. _____ _____ 襯衫 (2)   13. _____ _____ 大衣* (5)

4. _____ _____ 雜誌 (50)   14. _____ _____ 中文書 (26)

5. _____ _____ 裙子 (4)   15. _____ _____ 褲子 (1)

6. _____ _____ 哥哥 (3)   16. _____ _____ 老師 (7)

7. _____ _____ 書店 (8)   17. _____ _____ 圖書館 (2)

8. _____ _____ 大夫 (12)   18. _____ _____ 朋友 (13)

9. _____ _____ 銀行 (23)   19. _____ _____ 系 (46)

10. _____ _____ 宿舍 (55)   20. _____ _____ 學院 (20)

Exercise X (Cont.)

F. 問答 Answering Questions: Answer the following questions according to the information provided in the lesson and the actual situations about yourself.

1. 王老師給古波兩張甚麼票？

2. 古波和帕蘭卡晚上去作甚麼？他們從哪兒去？

3. 帕蘭卡穿哪件襯衫,哪條裙子去？

4. 你有幾件襯衫？

5. 帕蘭卡有沒有白裙子？你呢？

6. 你的上衣*是綠的嗎？

7. 你的襯衫都是新的嗎？

8. 你妹妹常穿新裙子嗎？

9. 你常去你老師家看他嗎？

10. 你們去哪兒買筆？從哪兒去？

Exercise XI
(Lesson 17)

A. 翻譯 **Translation**: Apply the illustrated pattern to translate the sentences into Chinese.

Pattern # 13a: **Supplementary pattern to #13: Position of Time-word**

	Subject NP	**Time-expression** Actual/Relative Time	**Predicate** + V +
[Example]:	我朋友	十二點一刻	來我家看我.

	Time-expression Actual/Relative time	**Subject** NP	**Predicate** + V +
[Example]:	下課以後	他們	去看京劇.

1. I go to class at 8:00.

2. I get out of class at a quarter past four.

3. I don't have anything in particular to do after class.

4. Please wait for me after class.

5. Shall we go to a movie together at seven o'clock?

6. See you at 6:30.

7. I'll wait for you at the movie theatre* at a quarter to seven, O.K.? [*=supplementary word.]

8. Shall we go to a coffee shop after seeing the movie?

9. We will go back to the dormitory after having (drunk) some coffee.

10. Good-bye. See you in the evening.

Exercise XI (Cont.)

B. 翻譯 **Translation**: Apply the illustrated pattern to translate the sentences into Chinese.

Pattern #27: **Time-expression used as modifier**

Subject			Predicate	
NP-Time	的	NP	V +	(Obj.: NP-Time 的 NP)
[Examples]: 七點鐘	的	課	太早.	
我們			看	八點半的電影.

1. I am going to a nine o'clock class.

2. I'll take the 8:40 bus to go to the Foreign Language Institute.

3. She is not going to see the 12:00 movie, but she will see the one at 2:00.

4. We are buying movie tickets. I am getting one for the 4:45 show and he is getting one for the 6:15 show.

5. I am not going to see the 9:30 p.m. Beijing Opera. The 9:30 show is too late [=wan3].

6. They both take the 10:05 bus to return to the dormitory.

7. I am waiting for the 11:25 bus.

8. Are you taking the 2:30 French class?

9. The morning classes all have too many people.

10. We have three Chinese language classes. Mr. Wang teaches the 8:10 class; Mrs. Gu teaches the 9:10 class; Miss Xie teaches the one at 10:10. [You may want to try to use the Chinese characters for the names. Also, don't forget to use the Chinese way of calling teachers.]

Exercise XI (Cont.)

C. 詞序 **Word order:** Rearrange the elements of each entry to make a grammatical sentence.

1. 半　　　點　　　四　　　　下課　　　我們

2. 我　　　不　　　看　　　京劇　　　去　　　　晚上

3. 一刻　　六點　　他　　　我　　　等　　　在　　　食堂

4. 八點　　二十分　上課　　他們

5. 以後　　下課　　宿舍　　我　　　回

6. 電影　　幾點　　的　　　看　　　我們

7. 他　　　上課　　常　　　坐車　　去

8. 去　　　咖啡館　我們　　走

9. 車　　　三點半　坐　　　去　　　我　　　圖書館　的

10. 我　　　我姐姐　咖啡　　一起　　去　　　跟　　　喝

Exercise XI (Cont.)

D. 用詞 Choice of Words: Fill in the blanks with the most appropriate words, using one character for each blank.

1. 我 ＿＿＿ 我朋友一起 ＿＿＿ 看電影.

2. 請你六 ＿＿＿ 半 ＿＿＿ 宿舍等我.

3. 下課 ＿＿＿ 後我 ＿＿＿ 家.

4. 我們 ＿＿＿ 車 ＿＿＿ 書店 ＿＿＿ 書.

5. 他們去 ＿＿＿ 九點一刻 ＿＿＿ 電影.

6. 我七 ＿＿＿ 二十分回宿舍 ＿＿＿ 信.

7. 我們不 ＿＿＿ 車去, 我們 ＿＿＿ 去.

8. 您晚上 ＿＿＿ 事兒嗎? 我 ＿＿＿ 看您, 好嗎?

9. 我八 ＿＿＿ 鐘 ＿＿＿ 前*沒有課.

10. 現在 ＿＿＿ 五分兩 ＿＿＿.

Exercise XI (Cont.)

E. 問答 **Answering Questions:** Answer the following questions according to the actual situations about yourself.

1. 請問,你幾點鐘上課?

2. 下課以後,你有事嗎?

3. 晚上九點以後,你在家嗎?

4. 下課以後,你常去喝咖啡嗎?

5. 你常跟誰一起去喝咖啡?

6. 你也常跟他一起去看電影嗎?

7. 你坐車去書店買書嗎?

8. 請問,晚上你幾點回宿舍?

9. 你回宿舍以後作甚麼?

10. 晚上請你在食堂等我,好嗎?

Exercise XI (Cont.)

E. 時間 Telling Time: Give one or two versions for each of the following:

_____   _____   _____

_____   _____   _____

_____   _____   _____

_____   _____   _____

Exercise XII
(Lesson 18)

A. 翻譯 **Translation**: Apply the illustrated pattern to translate the sentences into Chinese.

Pattern #28: **Narrative Sentence**: Using the expression "每 + Measure-word... (都)" to indicate routine or persistent activities and situations.

Someone	everyday / every time-unit	does this.
Subj.: person <-->	每(+) + Time unit	(都) Predicate
[Examples]: 他	每天	六點鐘起床.
古波	每天上午	都 去看他女朋友.

Pattern #29: **Narrative Sentence**: Using the expression "有時候" to indicate occasional events.

Occasionally	someone	does this.
有時候 <-->	Subj.: person	Predicate
[Example]: 有時候	我們	在宿舍看電影.

Note: **A <--> B** indicates that the positions of A and B may be switched.
These two patterns, #28 and #29, may also be applied to other situations with non-personal subjects. For example: "圖書館每天都有人." "有時候他的問題很多." In Pattern #28, with the word "都" the sentence emphasizes the consistency of an action. Without the word "都" the sentence refers to a normal daily routine.

1. I have classes every morning.

2. She sometimes has classes in the afternoon as well.

3. He always [=everyday, consistently] takes the bus to come here.

4. She goes to the college every day at a quarter past seven.

5. Every day after class she goes to the library to read.

6. Sometimes she does not eat in the dining hall.

7. Every evening [= Everyday's evening] after dinner she writes letter to her parents.

8. Occasionally she goes to see a movie with her friends.

9. Occasionally she also goes to the teacher's house to ask questions.

10. He sometimes eats after 6:00 p.m. and sometimes before* 6:00 p.m. [*=supplementary word]

Exercise XII (Cont.)

B. 詞序 Word order: Rearrange the elements of each entry to make a grammatical sentence.

1. 你　　　起床　　　幾點鐘　　每天

2. 我們　　課　　　　有　　　　每天　　　都

3. 他　　　都　　　　很多　　　有　　　　問題　　　每天

4. 以後　　下課　　　食堂　　　去　　　　吃飯　　　他們

5. 他們　　詞典　　　兩本　　　每個人 * (each person)　　有

6. 有　　　每個系 * (each department)　　　都　　中國留學生　　文學院

7. 每天　　以後　　　十二點　　睡覺　　　她

8. 上午　　問題　　　問　　　　我　　　　那兒　　　老師　　　去

9. 她　　　這兒　　　北京*　　　學習　　　漢語　　　去　　　　從

10. 我　　　有時候　　有時候　　在宿舍　　休息　　　在閱覽室 看報

Exercise XII (Cont.)

C. 用詞 Choice of Words: Fill in the blanks with the most appropriate words, using one character for each blank.

1. 她 _____ 天 (every day) 六點半 _____ 床 (gets up) .

2. 他們每天 _____ 有中文課 .

3. 他的每件大衣 (*every overcoat) _____ 是黑的 .

4. 我 每_____ 晚上 _____ 在圖書館看書 .

5. 謝老師給我們 _____ 個學生兩 _____ 中文雜誌 .

6. 我有時候十一點半睡覺, _____ _____ _____ 十二點(鐘) _____ _____ .

7. 他常去 _____ 那兒 _____ 問題 ?

8. 我 _____ 王老師兩 _____ 問題 .

9. 吃飯 _____ _____ 我想 _____ 他一起 _____ 閱覽室 _____ 報 .

10. 晚上我有時候跟朋友 _____ _____ 去看電影, _____ _____ _____ 在宿舍學習 .

Exercise XII (Cont.)

D. 問答 Answering Questions: Answer the following questions according to the information given in the textbook.

1. 丁雲是哪個系的學生？

2. 他們系有很多中國留學生嗎？

3. 英語系的中國留學生都住在哪兒？

4. 丁雲每天幾點鐘起床？幾點鐘睡覺？

5. 她每天都有課嗎？

6. 她幾點上課？幾點下課？

7. 她在哪兒吃飯？

8. 她幾點去閱覽室看報？

9. 她下午還作甚麼？

10. 她晚上作甚麼？

Exercise XIII
(Review L. 13-18)

A. 用詞 Choice of Words: Fill in the blanks with the most appropriate words, using one character for each blank.

1. "＿＿＿ 問,古波 ＿＿＿ 哪兒?" "他 ＿＿＿ 丁雲 ＿＿＿ 兒."

2. 他 ＿＿＿ 宿舍 ＿＿＿ 朋友＿＿＿ 信.

3. 你們認識 ＿＿＿ ＿＿＿ ＿＿＿ 張老師?" "我們＿＿＿ 不認識他."

4. "他去 ＿＿＿ ＿＿＿ 還書?" "他去帕蘭卡 ＿＿＿ 還書."

5. 他們 ＿＿＿ 學院去商店 ＿＿＿ 甚麼?

6. 你跟 ＿＿＿ 一起去 ＿＿＿ 京劇? 你們 ＿＿＿ 車去嗎?

7. "你買 ＿＿＿ ＿＿＿ ?" "我 ＿＿＿ 兩 ＿＿＿ 襯衫,一 ＿＿＿ 裙子, 兩 ＿＿＿ 書, ＿＿＿ 三 ＿＿＿ 京劇票."

8. 下午 ＿＿＿ 課 ＿＿＿ 後我 ＿＿＿ 跟朋友 ＿＿＿ ＿＿＿ 去咖啡＿＿＿ 喝咖啡. 晚上我 ＿＿＿ ＿＿＿ ＿＿＿ 去圖書館 ＿＿＿ ＿＿＿ 有時候 ＿＿＿ 家休息.

9. 晚上我們 ＿＿＿ 看七 ＿＿＿ 半 ＿＿＿ 電影.你 ＿＿＿ ＿＿＿ ＿＿＿ ?

10. "＿＿＿ 問,現在 ＿＿＿ ＿＿＿ ?" "＿＿＿ 十 ＿＿＿ 兩點."

Exercise XIII (Cont.)

B. 作文 **Composition:** Write a series of questions asking your friend about the Chinese department of his/her school.

C. 作文 **Composition:** Write a passage about your schedule for a normal school day.

Exercise XIII (Cont.)

Exercise XIII (Cont.)

D. 作文 Composition: A Note to a Blind Date: Your good friend Randy has set up a blind date for you but it's up to you to decide on the details. So, you are going to ask Randy to give a note to your blind date. In the note you are going to ask your date to meet you at a certain time and a certain place. You are also going to tell your date what kind of car you will be driving, what clothes you will be wearing, and may be even something you are going to carry with you just to further help your date to identify you. (Of course, this may also be used as a note to prepare yourself for a telephone conversation with your date before you meet.)

Exercise XIV
(Lesson 19)

A. 翻譯 **Translation**: Apply the illustrated pattern to translate the sentences into Chinese.

Pattern #30b: **Interrogative Sentence**: Using <是... 還是...> structure to inquire about choices or relative degree -- on the predicate.

+_____	**The subject**	**is**	**(doing / like) this**	**or**	**(doing/like) that?**
	Subj.	(是)	Pred. A	還是	Pred. B
[Examples]:	他	是	學生	還是	老師?
	你們	(是)	去看電影	還是	回宿舍?
請告訴我	她	(是)	三點(鐘)來	還是	四點(鐘)

1. Do you like classical music or popular music.

2. Do you like to drink jasmine tea or black tea?

3. Is this a French folk song or a German [=De2guo2 德國] folk songs?

4. Does your friend live in a dormitory or live at home?

5. I don't know whether he wants a glass of beer or a bottle of beer.

6. Was the attendant at the Coffee Shop male or female?

7. Do you want to buy apples* or oranges? [*=supplementary word]

8. Do you prefer to sing songs or listen to them [=to listen to songs]?

9. Is the classical music dictionary in the library or at the reading room?

10. Is your teacher's family name Bai or Zhang?

Exercise XIV (Cont.)

B. 翻譯 **Translation**: Apply the illustrated pattern to translate the sentences into Chinese.

Pattern #30b: **Interrogative Sentence**: Using <是... 還是...> structure to inquire about choices or relative degree -- on the subject.

	Is	**A (doing this/ more like this)**	**or**	**B doing this / more like this**?
	(是)	Subj. 1 (Pred.)	還是	Subj. 2. Pred.
[Examples]:	是	你	還是	你朋友去買票?
		大夫 忙	還是	老師 忙?

1. Is the green shirt or the white shirt newer?

2. Are you or your friend ordering an orange juice?

3. Is French wine* or American wine* tastier?

4. Is Mr. Xie [=Xie4 Lao3shi1] or Mrs. Gu [=Gu3 Lao3shi1] teaching you Chinese grammar?

5. Which do you think are more pleasant to listen to, folk songs or modern popular songs?

6. Is her older sister or her younger sister prettier?

7. Who do you think is better looking, the book shop attendant or the coffee shop attendant?

8. Is it going to be Miss Wang or Mr. Ma who teaches us to sing folk songs?

9. Who wants to buy the flower vase* [=bottle], you or your older brother?

10. Are you coming to my place to see him or should he go to your house to see you?

Exercise XIV (Cont.)

C. 詞序 Word order: Rearrange the elements of each entry to make a grammatical sentence.

1. 要　　橘子水　　杯　　一　　我

2. 喝　　紅茶　　喜歡　　不　　你　　嗎

3. 要　　要　　紅茶　　花茶　　你　　還是

4. 聽　　喜歡　　還是　　你們　　現代音樂　古典音樂

5. 請　　啤酒　　一瓶　　我　　給

6. 我　　唱片　　兩　　買　　要　　張

7. 我　　好嗎　　你　　教　　中國　　民歌　　請

8. 在　　音樂　　宿舍　　我們　　晚上　　聽

9. 他　　的　　聽　　別

10. 喝　　咖啡　　中國人　　不　　都　　喜歡

Exercise XIV (Cont.)

D. 用詞 Choice of Words: Fill in the blanks with the most appropriate words to make the passage a logical dialogue in a cafeteria, using one character for each blank.

服務員：" 小姐, 您 ＿＿＿＿ 甚麼?"

帕蘭卡：" 我 ＿＿＿＿ 一 ＿＿＿＿ 橘子水."

服務員：" 對不起, 我們没有 ＿＿＿＿ ＿＿＿＿ ＿＿＿＿. 我們有茶 ＿＿＿＿

　　　　咖啡. 您 ＿＿＿＿ 茶 ＿＿＿＿ ＿＿＿＿ (＿＿＿＿) 咖啡 ?"

帕蘭卡：" 你們有 ＿＿＿＿ ＿＿＿＿ 茶 ?"

服務員：" 有 ＿＿＿＿ 茶, 有 ＿＿＿＿ 茶, 也有 ＿＿＿＿ 茶 ."

帕蘭卡：" 我 ＿＿＿＿ 一 ＿＿＿＿ 紅茶."

服務員：" 先生, 您 ＿＿＿＿ ? 您也 ＿＿＿＿ 紅茶嗎 ?"

古波：" 你們 ＿＿＿＿ ＿＿＿＿ ＿＿＿＿ 啤酒 ?"

服務員：" 我們 ＿＿＿＿ 中國啤酒 ＿＿＿＿ 有德國啤酒."

古波：" ＿＿＿＿, 我 ＿＿＿＿ 一 ＿＿＿＿ 中國 ＿＿＿＿ ＿＿＿＿."

Exercise XIV (Cont.)

E. 問答 **Answering Questions:** Answer the following questions according to the actual situations about yourself.

1. 你喜歡聽音樂嗎？

2. 你喜歡聽音樂還是喜歡看書？

3. 你的朋友都喜歡古典音樂嗎？

4. 你要不要學唱中國民歌？

5. 你要誰教你唱中國民歌？

6. 我們請我們的音樂老師教我們，好嗎？

7. 你想是中國民歌好聽還是美國民歌好聽？

8. 你有中國歌的唱片＊嗎？

9. 你的古典音樂唱片＊多還是現代音樂唱片＊多？

10. 是你的唱片＊多還是你媽媽的唱片＊多？

Exercise XV
(Lesson 20)

A. 翻譯 Translation: Apply the illustrated pattern to translate the sentences into Chinese.

Pattern #31: **Ascriptive Sentence**: Using Verb-of-identification to indicate dates and time

	(a)	**This date/time**	**is**	**a day/time with this description.**
		Subj.	V-id	Complement
		NP-calendar date/sequential time	是	NP-calendar date/clock time
[Example]:		今天	是	十一月二十五號.

	(b)	**This date/time**	**is**	**that of this timely event.**
		Subj.	V-id	Complement
		NP-calendar date/sequential time	是	NP-Timely or listed event(s)
[Example]:		下星期四	是	他哥哥的生日.

	(c)	**This event**	**is**	**at this time.**
		Subj.	V-id	Complement
		NP-Event	是/是在	NP-calendar date/clock time
[Example]:		舞會	是(在)	八點鐘.

1. "What's today's date?" [=Today is what month, what day?]   "Today is December 3rd."

2. "What day (of the week) is today." [=Today is what day (of the week)?]   "Today is Tuesday."

3. "Is this year's October 1st a Saturday?" [Can you also answer this question in Chinese?]

4. "When is the Department's party [=evening party]?" "(It) is at 8:30 tonight [=today evening]."

5. After Sunday is Monday.

6. The tutorial class is at 3:15 p.m.

7. Is this year 1993?

8. Both of their birthdays are in September.

9. My afternoon class is at 12:20 and his is at 2:00.

10. This month is February. Afterwards (it) is March.

71

Exercise XV (Cont.)

B. 詞序 Word order: Rearrange the elements of each entry to make a grammatical sentence.

1. 有　　　下午　　　課　　　今天　　　我

2. 我　　　問題　　　兩個　　　有

3. 是　　　十九號　　　六月　　　生日　　　他的

4. 空兒　　晚上　　　今天　　　我　　　沒有

5. 現在　　有事兒　　您　　　嗎

6. 很　　　有意思　　學習　　語法

7. 舞會　　不參加　　他　　　的　　　中文系

8. 老師　　輔導　　我們　　給　　七點鐘　　晚上

9. 十月　　星期四　　是　　　嗎　　　二十七號

10. 一九九三年　　不是　　十五號　　三月　　今天

Exercise XV (Cont.)

C. 用詞 Choice of Words: Fill in the blanks with the most appropriate words, using one character for each blank.

1. 張老師兩點有課 _____ _____ 兩點半有課？

2. 今天 _____ 她十八_____ 的生日.

3. 他 _____ (requests) 老師 _____ 他們輔導.

4. 我下午沒課，我 _____ 空兒.

5. 他的同學都不 _____ _____ 他 _____ 的地址.

6. 他的生日是 _____ 九 _____ 七 _____.今年他二十一 _____.

7. 星期日我家 _____ 一個舞會.歡迎你們 _____ _____.

8. 他說舞會 _____ _____ 意思.他不 _____ 加.

9. "星期三我 _____ 你看電影,你有空兒去嗎？" "謝謝你,我有
   _____ _____.我 _____ _____ 去."

10. 他九 _____ 一刻來 _____ 我們輔導.

Exercise XV (Cont.)

D. 問答 **Answering Questions:** Answer the following questions according to your real-life situations.

1. 今天是幾月幾號? 星期幾?

2. 請問現在幾點?

3. 你的生日是哪一天? 你今年的生日是不是在星期六?

4. 今天的語法, 你有問題嗎?

5. 你常去聽音樂會嗎?

6. 音樂會有意思嗎?

7. 星期日你有空兒嗎?

8. 音樂老師的生日舞會你去不去參加?

9. 你知道不知道那個舞會是哪天?

10. 你知道音樂老師家的地址嗎?

Exercise XV (Cont.)

E. 問答 Answering Questions: Answer the following questions based on the illustrated calendar and the real-life situation. The day highlighted is the day when Wang San's younger brother was born.

```
┌─────────────────────────────────────┐
│              1 9 9 2                  │
├─────────────────────────────────────┤
│                                  1    │
│   2    3    4    5    6    7    8     │
│   9   10   11   12   13   14  15     │
│  16   17   18   19   20   21   22     │
│  23   24   25   26   27   28   29     │
├─────────────────────────────────────┤
│            F e b r u a r y           │
└─────────────────────────────────────┘
```

1. 王三(的)弟弟的生日是幾月幾號？

2. 王三的弟弟今年幾歲？

3. 今年是一九九二年嗎？

4. 一九九二年的二月有多少天？一九九三年呢？

5. 一九九二年的二月一號是星期幾？

6. 今年的二月十號是星期一嗎？二十五號呢？

7. 一九九二年的二月有幾個星期六？星期天呢？今年呢？

8. 王三弟弟的生日都是在星期六嗎？

Exercise XVI
(Lesson 21)

A. 翻譯 Translation: Apply the illustrated pattern to translate the sentences into Chinese.

Pattern #32a: Complex Sentence with Clause as Modifier: To give additional information on the predicate.

> **Note:** This type of sentence may be viewed as combining two sentences of common object.
> Sub-sentence #1: Subj.1+V.1+Obj. 他喜歡喝酒. (He likes to drink wine.)
> Sub-sentence #2: Subj.2+V.2+Obj. 我送他一瓶酒. (I give him a bottle of wine.)
> **New Sentences:**
> Subj. 1 + V.1 + (information from #2) 的 + Obj.
> 他喜歡喝我送他的酒. (He likes to drink the wine that I gave him.)
> Subj. 2 + V.2 + (information from #1) 的 + Obj.
> 我送他一瓶他喜歡喝的酒. (I gave him a bottle of wine that he likes to drink.)

1. We will all attend the dancing party he gives. [Note: to give a party = "kai1 wu3hui4"]

2. Many people like to read the magazines that the Chinese Reading Room does not have.

3. Please open the bottle of wine that your friend gave you.

4. All exchange students from Japan take the English Grammar course taught by Mr. Smith.

5. He is not drinking the orange juice he ordered.

6. We'll listen to the record* I bought at the Music Store [=Music Bookstore].

7. He is writing a letter to the friend who invited him for dinner.

8. He'll give some flowers (as presents) to his sister who works at the bank. It's her birthday today.

9. Today, she is wearing the green skirt her mother bought for her.

10. No one likes the movie that he recommended [=introduced] to us.

Exercise XVI (Cont.)

B. 翻譯 Translation: Apply the illustrated pattern to translate the sentences into Chinese.

Pattern #32b: Complex Sentence with Clause as Modifier: To give additional informarion on the subject.

> **Note:** This type of sentence may be viewed as combining two sentences of common subject.
>
> Sub-sentence #1:   Subj. + Pred. 1   王老師喜歡喝酒.
>
> Sub-sentence #2   Subj. + Pred. 2   王老師教我們漢語.
>
> **New Sentences:**
>
> Pred. 2 的 Subj. + Pred. 1   教我們漢語的王老師喜歡喝酒.
>
> Pred. 1 的 Subj. + Pred. 2   喜歡喝酒的王老師教我們漢語.

1. The exchange students who live in our dormitory all study English and French.

2. None of the teachers who teach us grammar lives in the foreign language Institute.

3. That bunch of flowers he gave me are very beautiful.

4. All of the dancing parties given by the Chinese Department are boring.

5. All of the foreign friends he introduced to me work in the bank.

6. The Japanese girls who come to the College to study are all very young.

7. The teacher who tutors us at night knows the address of the theatre.

8. The classes I attended this afternoon are all very interesting.

9. (Our) classmates who live in Room 406 wish you a happy birthday.

10. Miss Zhang, who works at the movie theatre, tells me that she'll come to see you at 8:30 tonight.

Exercise XVI (Cont.)

C. 詞序 **Word order:** Rearrange the elements of each entry to make a grammatical sentence.

1. 你　　　好　　　生日　　　祝

2. 學生　　年輕　　　的　　　那個　　　中國人　　是

3. 花　　　漂亮　　　真　　　束　　　這

4. 她　　　她媽媽　　像　　　真

5. 他們　　跳舞　　　不　　　那兒　　　在

6. 誰　　　帕蘭卡　　兩　　　電影　　　票　　　張　　　送

7. 跳舞　　喜歡　　　王太太　　不

8. 姑娘　　漂亮　　　很　　　都　　　日本　　　嗎

9. 門　　　請　　　開

10. 他　　我們　　　看看　　　去　　　吧

Exercise XVI (Cont.)

D. 用詞 Choice of Words: Fill in the blanks with the most appropriate words, using one character for each blank.

1. 你好! _____ 進, _____ 坐, _____ 喝茶.

2. _____ 你生日好!

3. 這 _____ 花是我朋友 _____ (給) 我的.

4. "你想, 是紅的花漂亮還是黃 _____ _____ _____ _____ ?"

   "紅的花漂亮, 黃 _____ _____ _____ (*even more) _____ _____ ."

5. 她的生日 _____ 九月六 _____ . 你的生日 _____ _____ _____ _____ _____ ?

6. "你妹妹今年 _____ _____ (or _____ _____)?" "她今年十 _____ ."

7. 他們在哪兒 _____ 舞?

8. 朋友 _____ (給) 他很多生日 _____* _____* (gifts). 他很 _____ _____ .

9. "他是日本人嗎?" "他不 _____ 日本人, 他 _____ 中國人 ."

10. 那個跳舞 _____ 姑娘 _____ 漂亮!

Exercise XVI (Cont.)

E. 問答 **Answering Questions:** Answer the following questions according to the actual situations about yourself or imagined situation.

1. 你今年多大？

2. 你的生日是哪一天？

3. 你是像你爸爸還是像你媽媽？

4. 你喜歡跳舞嗎？

5. 誰常送你花？你常送誰花？

6. 星期天在花店買花的人很多嗎？

7. 輔導你們漢語的老師是中國人嗎？

8. 你爸爸買的襯衫都很漂亮嗎？

9. 你大夫的那輛*車是不是日本車？

10. 他們都說書店的服務員很漂亮，你說呢？

Exercise XVII
(Lesson 22)

A. 翻譯 Translation: Apply the illustrated pattern to translate the sentences into Chinese.

<u>**Pattern #33**</u>: **Ascriptive Sentence:** Using Verb-exist. 在/有 or Verb-id 是 to indicate location.

電影院　　咖啡館　　飯館

書店　　銀行　　書店

	(a)	<u>This place</u>	<u>is at / is on</u>	<u>this location / this side.</u>	
		NP-place	V-exist	NP-position	
[Examples]:		電影院	在	那兒.	
		飯館	在	右*邊兒.	
	(b)	<u>Place A</u>	<u>is on</u>	<u>place B's</u>	<u>this side.</u>
		NP-place	V-exist	NP-place+ (的)	NP-position
[Example]:		電影院	在	咖啡館 (的)	左邊.
	(c)	<u>(On) place A's</u>		<u>this side</u>	<u>is</u>	<u>place B.</u>
		(V-ex) NP-place (+的)	NP-location	V-id	NP-place	
[Example]:		在咖啡館的	左邊	是	電影院.	
	(d)	<u>(On) place A's</u>	<u>this side</u>	<u>there is/are</u>	<u>this/these place(s).</u>
		(V-ex) NP-place(+的) NP-loc.	V-exist	(#+M) NP-place	
[Example]:		電影院	對面	有	兩個書店, 一個銀行.

<u>**Pattern #34**</u>: **Word-/Phrase-of-location used as modifier**

	+	<u>of this side/location</u>	<u>'s</u>	<u>person / thing</u>	+
		NP-position +	的	NP	
[Examples]:		左邊	的	人	是王老師.
	他住在	裏邊	的	房間.	
		上邊	的	兩本雜誌 很新.	

Note: In sentences of parallel clauses, the noun after 的 may be omitted if understood. Refer to Pattern #25 in Exercise (L. 16) and the following examples:

左邊的椅子很新, 右*邊的(椅子)也很新.
上邊的詞典是漢語詞典, 下邊的(詞典)是英漢詞典.

Exercise XVII (Cont.)

A. 翻譯 Translation: (Cont.)

1. Shirley's home is behind the Foreign Language College. It has more than ten rooms.

2. The study is on the lower level (and) their bedrooms are on the upper level. [Note: Conjunction is not needed in the Chinese sentence and 和 is certainly is not the right word for it here. Do you know why?]

3. Her bedroom is to the left of her younger sister's bedroom and to the right of her parents' (bedroom). Her bedroom is in the middle*.

4. To the right of her sister's bedroom is the bathroom.

5. Across from her bedroom, there is another [*use 還有] bathroom and next to it is a small room where no one lives.

6. The living room is next to the study and across from the dinning room.

7. There are two big chairs and three smaller chairs in the living room.

8. The coffee table is between the two big chairs.

9. In the dinning room, there are many chairs and a dinning table.

10. At the back of their house is a small garden. There are no flowers in the garden at this time.

Extra: Could you draw a picture illustrating Shirley's home based on the information provided in the preceding ten sentences?

Exercise XVII (Cont.)

A. 翻譯 Translation: (Cont.)

11. The inner rooms are bedrooms and the outer room is a study.

12. On the desk there are three books. The one on top is a grammar book; the one at the bottom is a world atlas; and the middle* one is the *Introduction to Chinese Folk Songs*.

13. Across from the study are two bedrooms. The one on the left is her bedroom and the one on the right is her brother's.

14. There are chairs both inside and outside* the living room. The ones inside are new ones and the ones outside* are old ones.

15. There are banks on both sides [=兩邊(兒)] of our house: a small one on the left and a large one on the right.

16. Winthrop's [*Can you make a Chinese name for Winthrop?] house has two gardens. The garden in the front does not have flowers, but the one in the back has many beautiful flowers.

17. The building across (from here) is a bookstore. The house to the right is my friend's home.

18. Let's go to the restaurant across (the street) to eat.

19. Are you going to the front reading room or the rear reading room?

20. Is he in the study upstairs [=on the upper (level)] or in the study downstairs [=on the lower (level)]?

Exercise XVII (Cont.)

B. 詞序 **Word order:** Rearrange the elements of each entry to make a grammatical sentence.

1. 厨房　　他們的　　大　　　　很

2. 有　　　花園　　一個　　　後邊

3. 我　　　卧室　　　的　　　　裏邊的房間　　　　是

4. 雜誌　　圖書館　　有　　　裏邊　　很多

5. 甚麼　　上邊　　　是　　　桌子

6. 電影　　的　　　　怎麼樣　　星期六

7. 茶　　　的　　　你的　　　是　　　　嗎　　　窗户*旁邊

8. 中間*　在　　　洗澡間　　兩個卧室

9. 洗澡　　在　　　上邊　　　洗澡間　　的　　　他

10. 書房　　卧室　　後邊　　　在

Exercise XVII (Cont.)

C. 用詞 Choice of Words: Based on the illustration (which is supposed to be the diagram of your house), fill in the blanks with appropriate words, using one character for each blank.

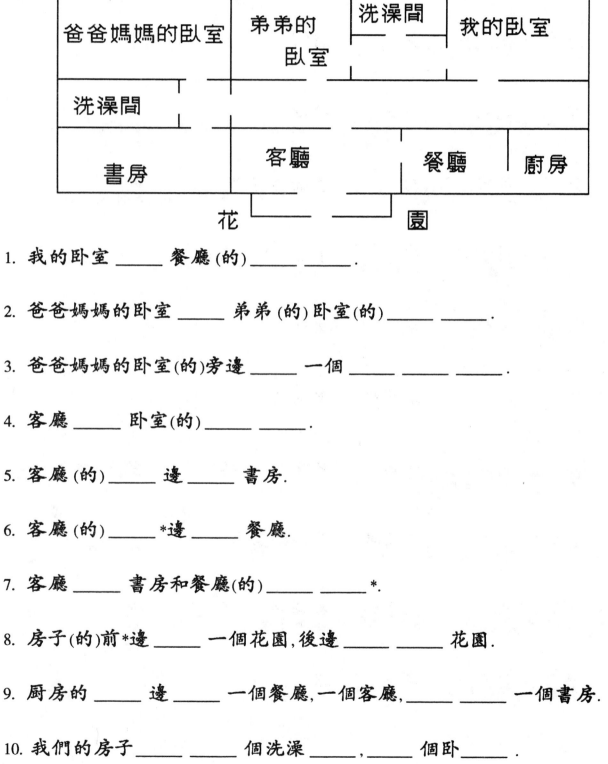

1. 我的臥室 ＿＿＿ 餐廳 (的) ＿＿＿ ＿＿＿ .

2. 爸爸媽媽的臥室 ＿＿＿ 弟弟 (的) 臥室 (的) ＿＿＿ ＿＿＿ .

3. 爸爸媽媽的臥室(的)旁邊 ＿＿＿ 一個 ＿＿＿ ＿＿＿ ＿＿＿ .

4. 客廳 ＿＿＿ 臥室 (的) ＿＿＿ ＿＿＿ .

5. 客廳 (的) ＿＿＿ 邊 ＿＿＿ 書房.

6. 客廳 (的) ＿＿＿ *邊 ＿＿＿ 餐廳.

7. 客廳 ＿＿＿ 書房和餐廳(的) ＿＿＿ ＿＿＿ *.

8. 房子(的)前*邊 ＿＿＿ 一個花園, 後邊 ＿＿＿ ＿＿＿ 花園.

9. 廚房的 ＿＿＿ 邊 ＿＿＿ 一個餐廳, 一個客廳, ＿＿＿ ＿＿＿ 一個書房.

10. 我們的房子 ＿＿＿ ＿＿＿ 個洗澡 ＿＿＿ , ＿＿＿ 個臥 ＿＿＿ .

Exercise XVII (Cont.)

D. 問答 Answering Questions: Suppose someone you know just bought a new house. Tell us about this house by answering the following questions.

1. 他們的新房子怎麼樣？

2. 他們的新房子後邊有沒有花園？前邊呢？花園裏邊有花嗎？

3. 他們的房子有幾個臥室？幾個洗澡間？臥室旁邊有沒有洗澡間？

4. 他們的客廳大不大？客廳裏邊有幾張桌子？幾把*椅子？

5. 他的臥室在哪兒？

6. 他的書房在哪兒？在客廳對面嗎？

7. 他總是在書房看書嗎？

8. 桌子上邊的書都是他的嗎？椅子上邊的呢？

9. 他常整理房間嗎？誰幫他整理房間？

10. 誰幫他們整理花園？

Exercise XVIII
(Lesson 23)

A. 翻譯 **Translation**: Apply the illustrated pattern to translate the sentences into Chinese.

Pattern #35: **Narrative Sentence:** Using (正)在+V-act ... (呢) to indicate action in progress.

	The subject	**is in the midst of**	**doing this**	**you know!**
	NP-person	(正)在	V-act (+Obj.)	(呢)
[Example]:	我們	正在	看電視	呢!
	The subject	**is right now**	**at this place**	**doing this**	**you know!**
	NP-person	(正)	在 + NP-pl	V-act (+Obj.)	呢
[Example]:	代表團	正	在工廠	訪問.

1. What are they doing now?

2. My mother is making a telephone call.

3. The delegation is paying a visit to the Chinese Department.

4. The delegate from the People's Daily* is interviewing [=訪問] our English teacher.

5. His younger brother is playing outside.

6. They are looking at the pictures.

7. We are watching the television news.

8. The workers are cleaning up [=putting things in order] the garden.

9. The Friendship Delegation is visiting an automobile factory.

10. She is reviewing the text of lesson 22.

Exercise XVIII (Cont.)

B. 翻譯 Translation: Apply the illustrated pattern to translate the sentences into Chinese.

Pattern #36: **Narrative Sentence**: Two actions with one in progress when the other takes place

	<u>The time when A takes this action,</u>	<u>B is in the midst of doing that.</u>
	NP1 V-act1 的時候	NP2 正/在/正在 V-act2
[Example]:	你 來 的時候,	我們 正在吃飯.

Note: Following is an illustration of the comparative time-span of the two actions.

[Action#1]
[_____ Action #2 _____]

1. When he came, we were eating dinner.

2. When you called, she was resting in her room.

3. I was looking for you when you came.

4. She was waiting for you when you came to pick her up.

5. When I saw you, you were talking with the factory workers.

6. When we went to the factory to visit, the workers were singing.

7. At the time when you get married, I will be visiting China.

8. When you entered the kitchen, we were helping mother cook.

9. When you called, I was just thinking of calling you.

10. When you were writing to her, she must also be thinking about you.

Exercise XVIII (Cont.)

C. 詞序 Word order: Rearrange the elements of each entry to make a grammatical sentence.

1. 他　　　休息　　　正在　　　嗎

2. 正在　　他們　　　報　　　看

3. 接　　　客廳　　　電話　　正在　　　她

4. 中國　　代表團　　在　　　訪問

5. 復習　　呢　　　我　　　課文　　在

6. 都　　　看　　　我們　　電視　　正在　　　呢

7. 正在　　她　　　你　　　等　　　家裏

8. 後邊　　她妹妹　　在　　玩兒　　房子

9. 正在　　寫信　　我　　　他　　來　　　的時候

10. 城裏　　代表團　　在　　工廠　　一個　　參觀

Exercise XVIII (Cont.)

D. 用詞 Choice of Words: Fill in the blanks with the most appropriate words, using one character for each blank.

1. 他們 ＿＿＿ 不 ＿＿＿ 家裏嗎？

2. 孩子們 ＿＿＿ ＿＿＿ 花園裏玩兒．

3. 你去接他的 ＿＿＿ ＿＿＿ 他 ＿＿＿ 在 ＿＿＿ 電話．

4. 你來 ＿＿＿ ＿＿＿ ＿＿＿ ，我們 ＿＿＿ 看電視新聞 ＿＿＿ ．

5. 代表團 ＿＿＿ ＿＿＿ 中國 ＿＿＿ ＿＿＿ ．

6. "喂！我 ＿＿＿ 小丁，請她 ＿＿＿ 電話." "好！請等 ＿＿＿ ＿＿＿ ."

7. 報上 ＿＿＿ 他們的照片 ＿＿＿ ＿＿＿ ？

8. 他們去看你 ＿＿＿ ＿＿＿ ＿＿＿ ，你在 ＿＿＿ 甚麼？

9. 誰 ＿＿＿ ＿＿＿ 聽音樂？(*who is listening to music at this time?)

10. 那個留學生 ＿＿＿ ＿＿＿ 城 ＿＿＿ 邊 ＿＿＿ ＿＿＿ 一個工廠．

Exercise XVIII (Cont.)

E. 問答 Answering Questions: Answer the following questions according to your real-life situation.

1. 你在作甚麼？

2. 誰在看報？他在哪兒看報？

3. 你爸爸媽媽在哪兒吃飯？

4. 你上課的時候，你的好朋友正在作甚麼？

5. 你復習課文的時候，有沒有人在看電視？

6. 你休息的時候，你的室友 (roommate) 在作甚麼呢？

7. 你去看你朋友他的時候，誰在他家？

8. 明天你有空嗎？

9. 我們去參觀咖啡工廠，好嗎？

10. 我們怎麼去呢？開車去嗎？

Exercise XIX
(Lesson 24)

A. 翻譯 Translation: Apply **all three** illustrated patterns to translate **each** of the sentences into Chinese.

Pattern #37: Interrogative Sentence Verifying a Statement

(a)	<u>Statement</u>_____ ,	是嗎?
[Example]:	她上課的時候很認真	是嗎?
(b)	<u>Statement</u>_____ ,	是不是?
[Example]:	你們每天上午鍛煉	是不是?
(c)	<u>Subj.</u>_____ 是不是	<u>Predicate</u> ?
[Examples]:	她	是不是	上課的時候很認真?
	她上課的時候	是不是	很認真?
	你們	是不是	每天上午鍛煉?

<u>Note:</u> (1) In pattern #37(c), the "...的時候" phrase may be grouped with the subject or the predicate as illustrated by the first and second sentences. The point of interrogation is, however, on what follows the expression "是不是." (2) Also review Patterns #2 and #15.

1. He likes to eat the dimsum his mother made, doesn't he?

2. Do you often practice Chinese together?

3. They are going to take a train to go to the rural area, aren't they?

4. Are they all enthusiastic when they do their physical training?

5. The new words that the teacher taught today are all very difficult, aren't they?

Exercise XIX (Cont.)

B. 詞序 Word order: Rearrange the elements of each entry to make a grammatical sentence.

1. 來　　　我家　　　你　　　玩　　　請

2. 古波　　去　　　火車　　農村　　坐　　　他爸爸　　看

3. 去　　　他們　　鍛鍊　　哪兒

4. 點心　　誰　　　作　　　是　　　那些　　的

5. 老師　　常常　　很難的　　我　　　問　　　問題

6. 吃　　　他媽媽　　點心　　他　　　給　　　作　　　常

7. 書　　　那些　　不是　　買　　　的　　　我

8. 他　　　正在　　打電話　　我　　　給我　　的時候　　鍛鍊

9. 他　　　這些　　京劇票　　是　　　都　　　買　　　的

10. 很　　　學習　　總是　　的時候　　她　　　認真

Exercise XIX (Cont.)

C. 用詞 Choice of Words: Fill in the blanks with the most appropriate words, using one character for each blank.

1. 她的家 _____ 城裏, 不 _____ 農 _____.

2. 她常常 _____ 火車 _____ 這兒玩兒.

3. 明天我 _____ 飛機 (fei1ji1, airplane) _____ 歐洲 (Europe*) _____ 朋友.

4. 這是我姐姐 _____ 你們作 _____ 點心.

5. 他現在很 _____ : 每天上午鍛 _____ , 下午工作, 晚上 _____
   學習漢語.

6. 我爸爸媽媽回家的 _____ _____ , 我 _____ 在 _____ 練習.

7. 我們 _____ 工廠 _____ _____ (*visit) 的時候, 工人都 _____ 休息.

8. 今天上課 _____ 時候, 老師 _____ _____ 我兩 _____ 問題.

9. 今天老師 _____ 的課文 _____ 語法我 _____ 不懂. 我沒(有)* (*did not)
   _____ _____ 老師 _____ _____ 問題.

10. 他是一個很 _____ _____ 的學生. 他學習 _____ 時候很 _____ _____ ,
    鍛煉 _____ _____ _____ 也很 _____ _____.

Exercise XIX (Cont.)

D. 問答 Answering Questions: Answer the following questions according to the actual situations about yourself and your own opinion.

1. 你的爸爸媽媽是農民嗎？

2. 誰的爸爸媽媽是農民？

3. 你每天都作語法練習嗎？

4. 你每天都鍛煉嗎？你甚麼時候鍛煉？

5. 你知道不知道你吃的飯是誰作的？是給誰作的？

6. 學漢語難不難？寫漢字呢？

7. 你朋友常來宿舍看你，是嗎？

8. 誰常去農村？他去那兒作甚麼？

9. 今天老師教的課文你懂不懂？

10. 你不懂的時候，你是不是問老師？

Exercise XX
(Review: L. 19-24)

A. 用詞 **Choice of Words:** Fill in the blanks with the most appropriate words, using one character for each blank. Note that the entries together form a story.

1. 小王說他女朋友明天＿＿＿ 城外邊＿＿＿ 火車＿＿＿ 看他.

2. 我 ＿＿＿ 小王她＿＿＿ 上午來＿＿＿ ＿＿＿ 下午來.

3. 小王 ＿＿＿ 他上午九＿＿＿ ＿＿＿ 去 ＿＿＿ 她.

4. 我不知道她來以後,＿＿＿ 住在小王 (＿＿＿)姐姐家＿＿＿ ＿＿＿ 住在學生宿舍.

5. 我 ＿＿＿ 小王他女朋友＿＿＿ ＿＿＿ ＿＿＿ 住在宿舍.
   他說不一定(*).

6. 我問小王＿＿＿ ＿＿＿ ＿＿＿ 很想他女朋友.

7. 他說他想她, 他 ＿＿＿ 想吃她作 ＿＿＿ 點心.

8. 我問小王:"你們在一起 ＿＿＿ ＿＿＿ ＿＿＿ , 她常 ＿＿＿ 你作點心＿＿＿ , ＿＿＿ ＿＿＿ ?"

9. 小王說:"我們 ＿＿＿ 一起 ＿＿＿ ＿＿＿ ＿＿＿ , 她常＿＿＿ 點心 ＿＿＿ 我＿＿＿ , 我＿＿＿ 常＿＿＿ 點心＿＿＿ 她＿＿＿ ."

10. 小王 ＿＿＿ 女朋友來的＿＿＿ ＿＿＿ , 我 ＿＿＿ ＿＿＿ 臥室＿＿＿ ＿＿＿ 看報. 小王＿＿＿ 我們介紹. 認識小王的女朋友我很＿＿＿ ＿＿＿ .

Exercise XX (Cont.)

B. 作文 Composition:

1. Write a passage about the things 謝文美 will do in August. During that month, her parents will be returning from their visit to Japan and the daughter of her parents' Japanese friend will come home with 文美's parents to study in the English department of her college. Later that month her younger brother will celebrate his birthday.

2. Write a passage about a telephone call you made to your sister/brother/friend. The two of you talked about the movie he/she saw recently, which you had recommended to him/her earlier. You also told him/her what you had been doing recently.

Exercise XX (Cont.)

C. 作文 **Composition:** Write a passage describing the following map.

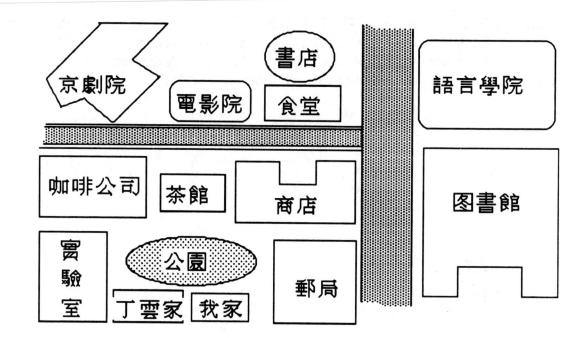

Exercise XX (Cont.)

D. 作文 Composition: Write a passage describing the following picture of 王三's bedroom.

Exercise XXI
(Lesson 25)

A. 翻譯 Translation: Apply the illustrated pattern to translate the sentences into Chinese.

Pattern #38: Narrative Sentence with Modifier Describing Manner of Action

	Someone	acts	in	this manner.
	NP	V-act	manner marker 得	Modifier-state
[Example]:	我	寫	得	很慢.

Note: No object of the verb is used in this pattern.

1. He sings well.

2. Ding Yun swims fast. [The word "游泳" may be analyzed as a Verb-Object combination.]

3. She studies diligently [=earnestly].

4. They have had a good time [=they played happily.]

5. They all came quickly.

6. We did not sleep well at night. [睡覺 may also be viewed as a Verb-Object combination.]

7. You worry [=think] too much.

8. She drives too fast.

9. Mr. Zhang teaches conscientiously.

10. You speak (Chinese) fluently*.

Exercise XXI (Cont.)

B. 翻譯 Translation: Apply the illustrated pattern to translate the sentence into Chinese.

Pattern #39: **Narrative Sentence with Modifier Describing Manner of Action -- Part 2**

	Someone	**in doing this**	**does (it)**	**in**	**this manner.**
	Subj.	Topic	Action	M-Marker	M-Modifier
	NP	V-act + Obj.	V-act	得	Adv.
[Example]:	我	寫字	寫	得	很慢.

Note: (1) This pattern includes a topic which in structure is a verb-object combination and in function is similar to a gerund in English. Since the topic is about the action, it includes the same verb as that for the action. (2) The positions of the subject and the topic may be switched. When the topic precedes the subject, the first verb may be omitted. Also, when the topic precedes the subject, the sentence may be called a "topical sentence." In a "topical sentence," the topic(s) is/are the focus of the sentence; a typical example is one involving listing, comparison or contrast such as the following:

(寫)字, 我寫得很慢, (説)話, 我説得很快.

1. She swims fast but her younger brother swims very slow.

2. We don't cook very well. She does?

3. As for teaching swimming, my coach does [=teaches] pretty well.

4. I ate too much fish.

5. They all speak Chinese clearly*.

6. He did not park correctly.

7. Those two young ladies drank too much soup.

8. Do you sleep very late?

9. She always prepares her lessons [use "text"] enthusiastically.

10. He dances beautifully but writes badly.

Exercise XXI (Cont.)

C. 詞序 **Word order:** Rearrange the elements of each entry to make a grammatical sentence.

1. 她   很快   游泳   得   游

2. 你們   得   飯   作   作   很不錯

3. 認真   鍛煉   很   我們   都   得

4. 今天   喝酒   喝   得   太多   你

5. 他   好不好   字   寫   得   寫

6. 請   停車   前邊   工廠   在

7. 吧   吃   麵包   再   一點兒

8. 爸爸   她(的)   (一)位   教練   是   游泳

9. 宿舍   河裏   游泳   後邊   在   他們   的

10. 他   我   請   喝   常   去他家   茶

Exercise XXI (Cont.)

D. 用詞 Choice of Words: Fill in the blanks with the most appropriate words, using one character for each blank.

1. 你吃 _____ 很少. _____ 吃點兒_____ !

2. 他說 _____ 太快. 我聽不 _____ _____ (clearly)*.

3. 他開車 _____ _____ 太快. 我不要他來 _____ 我. 我走去*.

4. 謝老師教漢語 _____ _____ 很 _____ _____ .

5. 他停車 _____ _____ 哪兒了?

6. 他媽媽常 _____ 魚湯 _____ 他 _____ .

7. 那 _____ 河的旁邊 _____ (一)個工廠.

8. 王蘭是我的 _____ _____ . 她教我游 _____ .

9. 他 (_____) 點心 _____ 得不錯, 我很喜歡 _____ .

10. 你 _____ 字 _____ _____ 真好!

Exercise XXI (Cont.)

E. 問答 Answering Questions: Answer the following questions according to the actual situations about yourself.

1. 你作飯作得好還是你爸爸作飯作得好？

2. 你寫字總是寫得很快嗎？

3. 你和你家人(your family)去玩兒的時候, 誰開車？誰準備吃的？

4. 誰開車開得好？誰作飯作得好？

5. 你媽媽是你的游泳教練, 是嗎？

6. 你晚上休息得好不好？

7. 今天教的課文, 你復習得怎麼樣了？

8. 你們教授教書*教得怎麼樣？

9. 你喜歡釣魚嗎？你常常去釣魚, 是不是？

10. 我吃奶酪吃得很少, 你呢？

Exercise XXII
(Lesson 26)

A. 翻譯 Translation: Apply the illustrated pattern to translate the sentences into Chinese.

Pattern #40: **Narrative Sentence:** Using potential markers 能/可以/想/要/會 to indicate
possibility.

Someone		may potentially	take this action.
NP	<neg.>	Potential Markers	VP
		能/可以/想/要/會	V-act + Obj.
[Examples]: 我		想	去日本.
我不知道甚麼時候		能 / 可以	去.
我去的時候		要	跟古蘭一起去.
她		會	説日語.

Note: The five potential-markers indicate different types of possibilities: 能 may indicate a general potential or a physical ability. 可以 implies permission, allowance, or agreement. 想 indicates a mental inclination while 要 presents a decision. 會 is a little different from the others; it may refer to a learned capability, a definite possibility or a strong prediction.

1. His mother wants him to be a doctor, but he doesn't want to be a doctor.

2. I don't know how to speak Japanese.   3. We are thinking of going to see a movie.

4. "Neither of us knows how to swim. Will you teach us?" "Sure [=no problem], I'll teach you."

5. His brother really knows how to cook.   6. Could you phone Professor Ding?

7. You are not allowed to fish in this river but you may fish in the river beside it.

8. "I would like to invite you over for dinner. Could you come?" "I'll certainly be there [=come].

9. In that college, students are not allowed to eat in the Professors' Dinning Hall.

10. I don't know how to drive. I want to learn. Will you teach me?

Exercise XXII (Cont.)

B. 詞序 Word order: Rearrange the elements of each entry to make a grammatical sentence.

1. 想   民歌   學習   你   哪國的

2. 理想   當   我的   老師   是

3. 去   想   游泳   他   不

4. 你   作家   研究   要   呢   哪位

5. 了解   我   中國   農村   問題   的   不

6. 當   當   你   不錯   得   翻譯

7. 研究   倆   他們   要   都   京劇

8. 那   有名   小説   很   本

9. 我   今天   明天   想去   或者   北京   就

10. 不   容易   翻譯   很   當   啊

Exercise XXII (Cont.)

C. 用詞 Choice of Words: Fill in the blanks with the most appropriate words, using one character for each blank.

1. 我以後想 _____ (to be a) 老師, 他 _____ _____ 大夫.

2. 我們再談 _____ 吧! 互相了解 _____ _____ .

3. 魯迅是一 _____ 有名的 _____ _____ .

4. 我們 _____ 想明年一月 _____ 去中國學習.

5. 翻譯 _____ _____ 能 _____ _____ 兩國人民的了解.

6. 以後我 _____ 學習法語 _____ _____ 日語.

7. 學生都 _____ _____ 認真學習.

8. 你以後想 _____ 甚麼工作? 我想你 _____ _____ 當作家.

9. 那個醫院有很多 _____ 名 _____ 大夫.

10. 研究中國文學不太難, _____ 不太 _____ _____ .

Exercise XXII (Cont.)

D. 問答 Answering Questions: Answer the following questions according to the actual situations about yourself.

1. 今天晚上你想作甚麼？

2. 以後你想作甚麼？你想當翻譯嗎？你會説法語或者德語嗎？

3. 你想是當翻譯有意思還是當教練有意思？

4. 談話能加深朋友的了解嗎？

5. 你會不會游泳？大學後邊兒的河裏可以不可以游泳？

6. 河旁邊能不能停車？

7. 從德國來的留學生回國以後作甚麼？

8. 你想去哪兒參觀？你會開車嗎？

9. 你想，找一個理想的工作容易嗎？

10. 你説，到中國去當翻譯，好不好？

Exercise XXIII
(Lesson 27)

A. 翻譯 **Translation**: Apply the illustrated pattern to translate the sentences into Chinese.

Pattern #41: **Narrative Sentence**: Using 了 (without quantitative measure) to indicate that an action has been initiated or (with quantitative measure) that an action has been initiated and reached a certain extent.

	The subj,	**has taken an action**	**and reached this level**	**on this.**
	NP	V-act + IM 了	Number + Measure	Obj.-NP
(a) [Examples]:	張小姐	來 了		
	我們	喝 了		湯.
	他	買 了	兩本	書.

	About this,	**someone has taken an action**	**and reached this extent.**
	Topic: NP	Subj.: NP + V-act + IM 了	Quantity: <#> <M>
(b) [Example]:	葡萄酒	我們 喝 了	一瓶.

Note: For more on "**Topical Sentence**," review notes on Pattern #39, Exercise XXI ((L. 25)

1. The movie has started.   2. We caught six fish.

3. I drank some grape wine and I also tasted a little Maotai.

4. At dinner [When I was eating dinner), I drank two cups of tea.

5. I bought some ham and cheese.   6. He answered the teacher's questions.

7. When I was in China, I became acquainted with two famous writers.

8. I have practiced the characters and I have also prepared the text.

9. The Chinese ambassador gave a reception.

10. I attended the embassy's cocktail party.

Exercise XXIII (Cont.)

B. 翻譯 Translation: Apply the illustrated patterns to translate the sentences into Chinese.

Pattern #42: **Narrative Sentence**: Using 沒(有) to indicate that an action has not been initiated.

(a)	**The subject**	**has not**	**taken an action**	**on this.**
	NP	Non-IM 沒(有)	V-act	Obj.-NP
[Examples]:	王參贊	沒有	參加	招待會.
	我	沒	問.	

(b)	**To this,**	**the subject**	**has not taken**	**this action.**
	Topic:NP	Subj.-NP	Non-IM 沒(有)	V-act
[Example]:	茅台酒	她	沒	嘗.

1. He did not translate those three words.

2. The attendant did not help us.

3. None of the members [=people] of the delegation came to the welcome party.

4. The coach did not teach us swimming.

5. She did not wear that red shirt I gave to her.

6. The Ambassador came but not his wife.

7. I ate some Chinese food [=dishes] but I did not use chopsticks.

8. He provided [=prepared] wine but he did not provide any mineral water.

9. We all tasted the Maotai but he did not.

10. He did not cook the rice and he did not cook any dishes. What do we eat?

Exercise XXIII (Cont.)

C. 翻譯 Translation: Apply the illustrated patterns to translate the sentences into Chinese.

Pattern #43: **Interrogative Sentence:** Using <V-act 了 ... 沒有 > structure to inquire if an action has taken place.

(a)	**The subject**	**has taken this action**	**or has not?**
	Subj.: NP	V-act + IM 了	Non-IM 沒有
[Example]:	大使夫人	來 了	沒有?
(b)	**The subject**	**has taken an action on this**	**or hasn't?**
	Subj.:NP	V-act IM 了 + Obj.	Non-IM 沒有
[Example]:	你們	學習了 中國文化	沒有?
(c)	**On this,**	**the subject** **has taken an action**	**or not?**
	Topic: NP	NP V-act + IM 了	Non-IM 沒有
[Example]:	中國文化	你們 學習 了	沒有?

Note: This pattern is similar to the "<+> <->" type of interrogative structure introduced by Patterns #15 and #17 in Exercises VII and VIII (L. 13 & 14). Other types of interrogative sentences, such as "Statement + 嗎," "the tag-question with 呢," etc.. may also be applied to narrative sentences the same way as they are applied to other types of sentences.

1. Has the movie started yet?

2. Did you buy any grapes?

3. Do you have any chopsticks?

4. Have you made the telephone call?

5. Did you try on that shirt?

6. Has the reception party started?

7. Did you invite the culture counselor and his wife?

8. Have you tasted that French brandy*?

9. Is everyone here yet? [Has everyone come?]

10. Has Madame Wang introduced you (plural) to each other?

Exercise XXIII (Cont.)

D. 詞序 Word order: Rearrange the elements of each entry to make a grammatical sentence.

1. 開始   還   招待會   沒有

2. 酒   喝   他   了   兩杯

3. 請進   都   你們   來了

4. 不   用筷子   會   太   我

5. 高興   我   認識   能   你們   非常

6. 參加   大使馆   大家   酒會   到   請

7. 乾杯   人民   兩國   爲   的   友誼

8. 筷子   留學生   兩位   會   都   這   用

9. 菜   作   作   好   很   他   得

10. 嘗嘗   菜   我弟弟   的   作   請

Exercise XXIII (Cont.)

E. 用詞 Choice of Words: Fill in the blanks with the most appropriate words, using one character for each blank.

1. 下午我們去飯館 _____ _____. 我們要 _____ 三 _____ 菜, 一 _____
   湯, 我們沒 _____ 酒.

2. 他 _____ 中國菜 _____ _____ 很好.

3. _____ 大家的健康 _____ 杯

4. 我上午 _____ 他 _____ 電話, 他不 _____ 家. 我想現在 _____ _____
   _____ _____ (...give it another try).

5. 筷子我會 _____ 了, 中國菜我 _____ 不會 _____.

6. 我去大使館 _____ _____ 了一 _____ 招待會, 喝 _____ 兩 _____
   茅台 _____. 還看 _____ 一 _____ 中國電影.

7. 能 _____ _____ 你的生日舞會, 我非常 _____ _____.

8. 我買 _____ 一 _____ 一九三六年 _____ 法國葡萄酒, 請大家 _____ _____.

9. 他今天作了很多事: 上午 _____ _____ 練習, 下午 _____ _____ _____
   房間, 晚上 _____ 作 _____ 飯. 可是他 _____ 寫信.

10. 這是中文 _____ 的教授王 _____ _____ 和 (他) _____ _____. _____
    教授 _____ 我們中國文學, _____ 夫人 _____ 大使館工作.

Exercise XXIII (Cont.)

F. 問答 **Answering Questions:** Answer the following questions based on the assumption that there a welcome party for the exchange students took place last week.

1. 歡迎留學生的招待會,誰去參加了?

2. 大家都去了嗎?

3. 招待會有甚麼酒?

4. 你可以不可以喝酒? 你會不會喝酒? 你喜歡喝酒嗎? 你喝了酒嗎?

5. 參加招待會的人都會用筷子嗎?

6. 中國大使館的文化參贊來了嗎? 你認識不認識他?

7. 你朋友問你:"那個魚湯是我作的. 你嘗了沒有?" 你怎麼回答?

8. 課文你復習了沒有? 生字都認識了嗎?

9. 招待會以後你們去看了電影嗎? 請了老師沒有?

10. 招待會以前誰去了大使館? 他去作甚麼?

Exercise XXIV
(Lesson 28)

A. 翻譯 **Translation:** Apply the illustrated pattern to translate the sentences into Chinese.

Pattern #44: **Narrative Sentence:** Using Initiation-Marker 了 to report on the occurrence of an event, or a new situation.

> **(a)**   <u>This event</u>   <u>has taken place</u>.
>
>   Sentence   IM 了
>
> [Example]:   我給我爸爸媽媽寫信   了.
>
> [Changed from a previous situation: 我(還)沒給我爸爸媽媽寫信.]
>
> **(b)**   <u>The subject</u>   <u>is no longer in this state</u>.
>
>   Subj.: NP   (Neg.) V-state/exist, etc. 了
>
> [Example]:   代表團   不在工廠了.
>
> [Change from a previous situation: 代表團在工廠.]

<u>Note</u>: (1) A 了 ("le") attached to the end of a sentence indicates that the event described in the sentence is supposedly a new situation to the listener. If it is attached to a positive statement, the sentence reports an event which has just taken place. If it is attached to a negative statement, the sentence means that the subject is no longer in the state described by the predicate. In either case, the sentence reports a new situation. Thus, in the example for Pattern #44 (a), the projected listener understood that prior to the statements, the subject had not yet written the letter. The statement is reporting a new situation: the subject has now written the letter. Similarly, in the example for (b), the subject's not being in the factory is a new situation. In other words, before the statement (b) was made, the projected listener's understanding was that the delegation was in the factory. Example for (b) informs the listener that the delegation has left and is no longer in the factory.
(2) While in this type of sentence the entire event is considered as a whole, in a sentence with "le" immediately following a verb of action the emphasis is on the action and the word "le" indicates the initiation of that action. It should be noted that "le" is not a "past-tense suffix." While the two types of sentences introduced in the previous lesson and this lesson may sometimes be translated into the same English sentence, each has a different emphasis.

1. The delegation has (now) come.

2. Guess what? [=Do you know?]   (Contrary to what you might have expected,) we went to see the football game!

3. When I lived at home, I did not like to eat cheese, but after I started living in the dormitory, I have come to like to eat cheese.

Exercise XXIV (Cont.)

A. 翻譯 Translation: (Cont.)

4. He is finally cleaning up his room.

5. "I bought a Chinese dictionary." "Really! You [finally] bought a dictionary!"

6. She is not our coach any more. She is now a volleyball*-game referee.

7. He has finally called us (on the telephone).   8. [Trust me!] I did give him the hat.

9. I have gone to the embassy to get the visa.   10. We may now go to the skating rink [=field].

11. The Chinese Department team has had a ping-pong* match with the Exchange Student team.

12. The Chinese Department team won [for a change!] .

13. My brother's friend has come. My brother is no longer angry.

14. They have gone to visit the shoe factory.   15. We don't have any question anymore.

16. He is no longer doing research on French literature; he is researching Chinese music now.

17. It is winter now. Those little children are not playing outside anymore.

18. Her younger sister has (now) learned to [=know how to] kick the ball.

19. She ate breakfast today [for the first time!].   20. The referee has finally come.

Exercise XXIV (Cont.)

B. 翻譯 Translation: Apply the illustrated pattern to translate the sentences into Chinese.

Pattern #45: Interrogative Sentence: Asking if the action has taken place-- Part 2

	The subject	**has or has not taken this action**			**to this object?**
	NP	V-act	没	V-act	NP
[Examples]:	他們	買	没	買	京劇票?
	他	整	没	整理	房間?

Note: This is an abbreviated form of Pattern #43. It is a general practice to use only the first character of the v-act word before 没.

1. Did he go to the embassy?

2. Did he participate in the football game?

3. Did the delegation visit the maotai factory?

4. Did you do (your) homework [=exercise]?

5. Did they go skating?

6. Has the movie started yet?

7. Did she answer the ambassador's questions?

8. Did they entertain [=招待] the counselor's wife?

9. Have you packed [=put the luggage in order] yet?

10. Did you all do (your) physical training?

Exercise XXIV (Cont.)

C. 翻譯 Translation: Apply the illustrated pattern to translate the sentences into Chinese.

Pattern #46: **Interrogative Sentence**: Asking if a new situation has taken pace.

	This new situation	has taken place	has (it) not?
	Sub.: NP + V-act + Obj.: NP	IM- 了	Non-IM 没有 ?
[Example]:	你去辦簽證	了	没有 ?

1. Have you had [=eaten] lunch yet?

2. Has the coach of the university team come yet?

3. Did he (finally) take care of the visa-application?

4. Did you watch the ball game last night (after all)?

5. Have you packed your suitcase?

6. Have you bought the skates?

7. Have you gone skating this winter?

8. Has her sister cooked breakfast yet?

9. Have all the referees left yet?

10. Has the football game started yet?

Exercise XXIV (Cont.)

D. 翻譯 Translation: Apply the illustrated pattern to translate the sentences into Chinese.

Pattern #47: **Narrative Sentence of Sequential Actions**

	Subj. A	**after completing act. 1**	**Subj. (A /) B**	**then**	**takes act. 2**
	Subj.: NP	V-act1 了 + Obj.	NP	就	V-act2 + Obj.
[Examples]:	我	打了電話		就	去大使館.
	他	買了書	我們	就	走.

1. Having entered the room, they drink some tea.

2. Having bought the tickets, they entered the theatre.

3. After I arrive in China, I'll go see the Great Wall.

4. After he packs, he'll leave.

5. After the ambassador gets here [=has come], the reception will starts.

6. After watching the ball game, they all returned home.

7. When(ever) they lose, his father will say that the coach is not good.

8. After you buy the skates, we can go skating.

9. You should pack right after you buy the suitcase.

10. After getting into the city, I'll go visit (our teacher) Mr. Zhang.

Exercise XXIV (Cont.)

E. 詞序 **Word order:** Rearrange the elements of each entry to make a grammatical sentence.

1. 他　　　簽證　　　辦　　　　大使館　　去

2. 跟　　　工廠隊　　農村隊　　足球　　　比賽

3. 帽子　　冰鞋　　　兩雙　　　一頂　　　我想買　　跟

4. 午飯　　就　　　　吃了　　　吧　　　　出發

5. 球隊　　的　　　　他們　　　贏了　　　比　　　六　　　九

6. 裁判　　總是　　　說　　　　公平　　　不　　　別

7. 我們　　電影　　　票　　　　了　　　　看　　　買　　　就去

8. 來　　　比賽　　　裁判　　　了　　　　開始　　就

9. 談　　　問題　　　你們　　　這個　　　沒談

10. 麵包　嘗了　　　你　　　　沒有　　　奶酪

Exercise XXIV (Cont.)

F. 用詞 Choice of Words: Fill in the blanks with the most appropriate words, using one character for each blank.

1. 昨天的球 _____ 大學 _____ 贏了, 二十 _____ 七.

2. 你復習 _____ 課文 _____ 去休息吧.

3. 你們隊輸 _____ 你 _____ 說 _____ _____ 不公平.

4. 他下 _____ 課 _____ 去踢 _____.

5. 我 _____ 了代表團 _____ 去 _____ _____ 招待會.

6. 我 _____ 了球賽 _____ 去 _____ 簽證.

7. 明天他要 _____ 大使夫人一起到 _____ _____ 場*去 _____ 網球*.

8. 我 _____ 去公園*滑冰, 可是我沒有 _____ 鞋, 我不能去 _____.

9. "你沒有冰鞋? 沒問題! 我 _____ 你一 _____ 吧!" "非常 _____ _____."

10. 昨天的藍球* _____, 我們隊贏了, 我真 _____ _____."

Exercise XXIV (Cont.)

G. 問答 **Answering Questions:** Answer the following questions according to the actual situations about yourself or imagined situations.

1. 你們昨天去城裏玩得怎麼樣？

2. 你喜歡打乒乓球還是喜歡踢足球？

3. 你買了冰鞋我們就去滑冰，好不好？

4. 昨天的藍球*友誼賽哪隊贏了？幾比幾？

5. 你們甚麼時候去吃午飯？ [Use "... 了 ... 就 ..."]

6. 你的箱子整理得怎麼樣了？

7. 昨天晚上你看電視了沒有？

8. 電視上的球賽怎麼樣？教練怎麼樣？裁判呢？

9. 你今天吃了早飯作了甚麼？

10. 你辦了簽證就去日本嗎？

Exercise XXV
(Lesson 29)

A. 翻譯 **Translation:** Apply the illustrated pattern to translate the sentences into Chinese.

Pattern #48: **Narrative Sentence:** Predicting a new situation that will soon take place

	The Subj.	**will soon**	**take this action.**	
	NP	要/快要/就快要/就要	V-act	了
[Examples]:	我們	就要	去滑冰	了.
	飛機	快要	到	了.
	足球賽	就快要	開始	了.

> **Note:** there is a slight difference among these four expressions in terms of degree of immediacy. The immediacy increases from 要 to 快要 to 就快要 to 就要.

1. We are going to a class soon.

2. Spring will soon be here [=come].

3. They are going to China soon.

4. I will soon pack my luggage.

5. We will soon use a new book.

6. We will soon go to the Embassy to get our visa.

7. The airplane will soon take off.

8. My classmates will come soon.

9. He'll be back soon. I am so happy!

10. The airplane will soon arrive in Beijing.

Exercise XXV (Cont.)

B. 翻譯 Translation: Apply the illustrated pattern to translate the sentences into Chinese.

Pattern #49: **Narrative Sentence**: Predicting a new situation to take place in the near future--with specific time indicated.

	The subj.	will at this time		take this action.
	NP	Time + 就/就要		V-act + 了
[Examples]:	王老師	明天	就要	離開 了.
	(中學)	一月三號	就	開始上課 了.
	飛機	兩點鐘	就	起飛 了.

Note: Since a specific time is indicated, the general time expressions 快要 and 就快要 become inappropriate in this pattern.

1. The airplane will take off as early as 5:30 p.m.

2. They will go to China as early as next summer.

3. He'll pick you up at 2:30 p.m.

4. We will leave our parents as early as this fall.

5. We will start using the new Chinese book next January.

6. I will write to my teacher this evening.

7. We'll arrive at the airport at 1:15.

8. Professor Wang will teach us Chinese folk songs this afternoon.

9. I'll go learn to drive tomorrow morning.

10. Classes will be over at 11:30.

Exercise XXV (Cont.)

C. 詞序 Word order: Rearrange the elements of each entry to make a grammatical sentence.

1. 明年　　中國　　去　　　看　　　我們　　他們

2. 平安　　你們　　一路　　祝

3. 開　　了　　　火車　　要　　　快　　　就

4. 去　　三點鐘　　接你　　機場　　一定　　我

5. 大家　　緊　　站(得)　　一點　　請

6. 身體　　注意　　要　　　也要　　學習　　努力

7. 就要　　離開　　了　　　所以　　他們　　很難過　　我

8. 健康　　你們　　祝　　　身體

9. 就　　你們　　吧　　　休息　　整理整理

10. 可是　　就要　　了　　　好朋友　　他們　　是　　分開

Exercise XXV (Cont.)

D. 用詞 Choice of Words: Fill in the blanks with the most appropriate words, using one character for each blank.

1. 他 _____ 去機場_____ 朋友,_____ _____ 不能來 _____ _____ 舞會.

2. 他媽媽_____ 他 _____ _____ 身體.

3. 明年秋 _____ 我 _____ 要去中國_____.

4. 請 _____ 我們_____ 一張相.

5. 他知道他 _____ _____ 離開了,_____ _____ 他不願 _____ 離開.

6. 飛機就要 _____ _____ 了, 請大家_____ 飛機吧

7. 別忘 _____, 到_____ 北京_____ 給我 _____ 信.

8. "我們非常感謝您." "_____ _____, 這是我 _____ _____ 作的."

9. _____ 難過! 我們很快 _____ _____ 見面了.

10. 李老師 _____ 書很認真,_____ _____ 學生學習得都很_____ _____.

Exercise XXV (Cont.)

E. 問答 **Answering Questions:** Answer the following questions assuming that you are about to take a trip to China.

1. 你去中國是夏天去還是秋天去?

2. 你要坐飛機去還是坐船*去?

3. 你是不是要坐飛機去?

4. 飛機幾點起飛?

5. 從你家去機場怎麼去? 坐火車去嗎?

6. 你爸爸媽媽去送你嗎? 他們身體怎麼樣?

7. 在機場誰要給你們照相?

8. 就要離開家了, 你難過嗎?

9. 你高興嗎? 爲甚麼 (for what, why)?

10. 你去中國以後要作甚麼?

Exercise XXVI
(Lesson 30)

A. 翻譯 Translation: Apply the illustrated pattern to translate the sentences into Chinese.

Pattern #50: **Descriptive Statement on Geographical Distance**

Place A	**is away from**		**Place B**	**by this much.**
NP-place	<--distance between--> 離		NP-place	Modifier-dist.
[Example]: 美國	離		中國	很遠.

Note: This very important pattern is introduced in Lesson 30 of *PCRI*. However, except for the two words 離 and 遠, no other vocabulary related to this pattern is introduced at the same time. Therefore, we are going to use the words about places previously introduced to practice this pattern. Maybe it is also a good idea to learn, ahead of the class plan of the textbook, the word for "close" 近 (jin4, to appear in lesson 44 of *Practical Chinese Reader*.)

1. England is not very far away from Germany.   2. Our house is not far from the bookstore.

3. Both the bank and the library are not far from the college.

4. That factory is not far from the river.   5. The airport is not very far from my house.

6. My bedroom is too far away from the bathroom.

7. Our classroom is too close to the football stadium (...場)

8. The airplane is far from us now.

9. The exchange students are far away from home. Therefore, they are quite homesick.

10. Is the embassy farther from the center of city or from the suburb? [Use 是 ... 還是...]

Exercise XXVI (Cont.)

B. 詞序 Word order: Rearrange the elements of each entry to make a grammatical sentence.

1. 離   日本   這兒   遠   很

2. 很   丁太太   難過   心裏

3. 他   他   笑了   很   高興

4. 贏了   很高興   我們   球賽   都   心裏

5. 宿舍   他的   圖書館   不遠   離

6. 給   女朋友   他   買了   他的   很多東西

7. 訪問   我們   歡迎   你   去   國家

8. 這兒   很好   我   過得   在

9. 學習   他爸爸   努力   他   要

10. 你   好嗎   送   回家   他   請

Exercise XXVI (Cont.)

C. 用詞 Choice of Words: Fill in the blanks with the most appropriate words, using one character for each blank.

1. 丁國安的家＿＿＿＿ 學生宿舍很遠.

2. 昨天他買 ＿＿＿＿ 一輛 (*measure for vehicles, pronounced "liang4") 車.

3. 買＿＿＿＿ 車 (以後) 他 ＿＿＿＿ 去買東西.

4. 他買＿＿＿＿ 很多＿＿＿＿ ＿＿＿＿ :他買了一 ＿＿＿＿ 鞋, 兩＿＿＿＿ 襯衫,
　　＿＿＿＿ 買＿＿＿＿ 一 ＿＿＿＿ 帽子.

5. 現在他有車＿＿＿＿ . ＿＿＿＿ ＿＿＿＿ 去上課的時候他不要他同學來
　　＿＿＿＿ 他, 他＿＿＿＿ ＿＿＿＿ 可以＿＿＿＿ 車去＿＿＿＿ .

6. 今＿＿＿＿ 夏 ＿＿＿＿ 他到外國去訪問＿＿＿＿ .

7. 他 ＿＿＿＿ ＿＿＿＿ 的那天, 他的朋友 ＿＿＿＿ 他去機場.

8. 丁國安離＿＿＿＿ 了. 他的好朋友小張 ＿＿＿＿ ＿＿＿＿ 非常＿＿＿＿ ＿＿＿＿ .

9. 丁國安還＿＿＿＿ 離開 ＿＿＿＿ 時候, 小張 ＿＿＿＿ ＿＿＿＿ 很高興. ＿＿＿＿
　　＿＿＿＿ 她常常＿＿＿＿ .

10. 丁國安 ＿＿＿＿ ＿＿＿＿ 以後, 小張不常常＿＿＿＿ 了. 她現在還常常
　　＿＿＿＿ . 每天都跟自＿＿＿＿ 說: "＿＿＿＿ 難過, 國安就＿＿＿＿ ＿＿＿＿
　　回來＿＿＿＿ ."

Exercise XXVI (Cont.)

D. 問答 Answering Questions: Answer the following questions according to the your real-life situations but also with the assumption that you are about to take a trip to China.

1. 機場離火車站*遠嗎?

2. 你家離圖書館遠還是離足球場遠?

3. 是大使館(離足球場遠)還是書店離足球場遠?

4. 你們漢語老師的家離中文系遠不遠?

5. 歡送會(* farewell party) 以後, 誰送老師回家?

6. 你去中國是跟老師一起去嗎? 你還要去甚麼國家?

7. 你去中國, 你爸爸媽媽放心嗎?

8. 你就要離開了, 誰心裏很難過? 誰給你買了很多東西?

9. 你在外國的時候會很想家嗎? 你會常哭嗎?

10. 你甚麼時候回國?

Exercise XXVII
(Review L. 25-30)

A. 用詞 Choice of Words: Fill in the each blank with an appropriate character to make the following two meaningful passages.

1. 明天是星期日,我想去釣魚.我也 ＿＿＿＿ 請我朋友跟我一起去.我給他打＿＿＿＿ 一個電話.問他＿＿＿＿不＿＿＿＿去釣魚.我朋友說他很 ＿＿＿＿ 去,可是他不＿＿＿＿ 去,他＿＿＿＿在家念書.我說明天是星期日.我們每天都念書,很＿＿＿＿.星期日＿＿＿＿＿＿＿＿休息休息,去玩玩.他說他知道我課文＿＿＿＿語法都會＿＿＿＿所以我＿＿＿＿＿＿＿＿去.可是他的語法＿＿＿＿有很多問題.他不＿＿＿＿去.我說我＿＿＿＿＿＿＿＿幫助他.今天晚上我＿＿＿＿＿＿＿＿跟他一起學習.他不懂的語法我們＿＿＿＿＿＿＿＿一起研究.他語法都懂＿＿＿＿他＿＿＿＿＿＿＿＿＿＿＿＿跟我一起去釣魚＿＿＿＿.他說,"好." 他問我＿＿＿＿不＿＿＿＿吃＿＿＿＿晚飯＿＿＿＿去他宿舍.我說:"好,我們晚上見."

2. 昨天晚上我 ＿＿＿＿ 大友一起去王家參加 ＿＿＿＿ 一個招待會.晚上六＿＿＿＿＿＿＿＿大友＿＿＿＿車來＿＿＿＿我.他開車＿＿＿＿＿＿＿＿很快.十五＿＿＿＿鐘＿＿＿＿到＿＿＿＿.所以,我們到＿＿＿＿很＿＿＿＿.那個招待會是為文大使開＿＿＿＿(招待會).參加＿＿＿＿人很多.大家都說中國話.大友說中國話＿＿＿＿＿＿＿＿很好.所以,他說＿＿＿＿很多＿＿＿＿,＿＿＿＿認識＿＿＿＿很多＿＿＿＿＿＿＿＿.大友＿＿＿＿我介紹＿＿＿＿幾＿＿＿＿朋友.我說中國話說＿＿＿＿不好.我不太＿＿＿＿說.我說＿＿＿＿時候常常＿＿＿＿＿＿＿＿不對.那些新朋友問＿＿＿＿我很多問題,可是我想我回答＿＿＿＿不太＿＿＿＿＿＿＿＿.我說話＿＿＿＿＿＿＿＿不多,可是喝酒＿＿＿＿＿＿＿＿很多.吃菜＿＿＿＿也不＿＿＿＿.王太太作菜＿＿＿＿＿＿＿＿非常＿＿＿＿.招待＿＿＿＿也很＿＿＿＿.我們回家＿＿＿＿＿＿＿＿很晚.我們都玩＿＿＿＿非常＿＿＿＿＿＿＿＿.

Exercise XXVII (Cont.)

B. 作文 Composition: Using approximately 150 characters to write a passage discussing your plans for the future.

C. 作文 Composition: Using approximately 150 characters to write a passage about your experience of seeing off a friend at the airport.

Character Finding lists

Pinyin	Character	Lesson
à	啊	13
ài	愛	14
ān	安	29
ba	吧	21
bā	八	11
bà	爸	4
bái	白	16
bān	班	20
bàn	半	17
bàn	辦	28
bāng	幫	22
bāo	包	25
bào	報	11
bēi	杯	19
bèi	備	25
běn	本	15
bǐ	筆	13
bǐ	比	28
biān	邊	22
biǎo	表	23
bié	別	19
bīng	冰	28
bù	不	3
bù	步	29
cái	裁	28

Stroke #	Character	Pinyin
1	〇	líng
1	一	yī
2	八	bā
2	二	èr
2	九	jiǔ
2	了	le
2	力	lì
2	七	qī
2	人	rén
2	十	shí
2	又	yòu
3	大	dà
3	大	dài
3	工	gōng
3	己	jǐ
3	口	kǒu
3	女	nǔ
3	三	sān
3	上	shàng
3	下	xià
3	小	xiǎo
3	也	yě
3	子	zǐ
4	不	bù
4	分	fēn

134

Pinyin	Character	Lesson	Stroke#	Character	Pinyin
cài	菜	27	4	夫	fū
cān	參	20	4	公	gōng
cān	餐	22	4	化	huà
céng	層	10	4	火	huǒ
chá	茶	8	4	今	jīn
chà	差	17	4	介	jiè
cháng	常	12	4	六	liù
cháng	嘗	27	4	日	rì
chǎng	場	29	4	少	shǎo
chǎng	廠	23	4	什	shén
chàng	唱	19	4	水	shuǐ
chē	車	5	4	太	tài
chèn	襯	16	4	天	tiān
chéng	城	23	4	文	wén
chéng	成	26	4	五	wǔ
chī	吃	18	4	午	wǔ
chū	出	23	4	心	xīn
chú	厨	22	4	友	yǒu
chuān	穿	16	4	月	yuè
chuáng	床	18	4	中	zhōng
cí	詞	11	5	白	bái
cóng	從	16	5	半	bàn
cūn	村	24	5	包	bāo
cuò	錯	25	5	本	běn
dá	答	24	5	比	bǐ
dǎ	打	23	5	出	chū
dà	大	5	5	打	dǎ
dài	大	5	5	代	dài
dài	代	19	5	冬	dōng
dài	待	27	5	古	gǔ

Pinyin	Character	Lesson
dāng	當	15
dǎo	導	20
dào	道	20
dào	到	27
de	的	5
dé	得	25
děng	等	17
dì	弟	3
dì	地	7
diǎn	典	11
diǎn	點	17
diàn	店	13
diàn	電	17
diào	釣	25
dǐng	頂	28
dìng	定	20
dōng	冬	28
dōng	東	30
dǒng	懂	24
dōu	都	3
duàn	鍛	24
duì	對	13
duì	隊	28
duō	多	10
ér	兒	10
èr	二	10
fā	發	23
fǎ	法	12
fān	翻	26
fàn	飯	18

Stroke#	Character	Pinyin
5	互	hù
5	加	jiā
5	叫	jiào
5	可	kě
5	民	mín
5	片	piàn
5	平	píng
5	去	qù
5	生	shēng
5	四	sì
5	他	tā
5	台	tai
5	外	wài
5	以	yǐ
5	用	yòng
5	正	zhèng
5	左	zuǒ
6	安	ān
6	冰	bǐng
6	成	chéng
6	吃	chī
6	地	dì
6	多	duō
6	行	háng
6	好	hǎo
6	回	huí
6	件	jiàn
6	老	lǎo
6	忙	mang
6	名	míng

Pinyin	Character	Lesson
fáng	房	22
fǎng	訪	23
fàng	放	29
fēi	啡	17
fēi	非	21
fēi	飛	29
fēn	分	17
fū	夫	5
fú	服	19
fǔ	輔	20
fù	復	23
gāi	該	26
gān	乾	27
gǎn	敢	15
gǎn	感	21
gāo	高	21
gào	告	14
gē	哥	3
gē	歌	19
gè	個	15
gěi	給	14
gēn	跟	17
gèng	更	21
gōng	工	14
gōng	公	28
gū	姑	21
gǔ	古	19
guān	觀	23
guǎn	館	15
guì	貴	9

Stroke#	Character	Pinyin
6	奶	nǎi
6	年	nián
6	她	tā
6	同	tóng
6	西	xī
6	先	xiān
6	行	xíng
6	休	xiū
6	有	yǒu
6	在	zài
6	再	zài
6	早	zǎo
6	字	zì
6	自	zì
7	吧	ba
7	別	bié
7	步	bù
7	車	chē
7	床	chuáng
7	村	cūn
7	弟	dì
7	告	gào
7	更	gèng
7	見	jiàn
7	究	jiū
7	快	kuài
7	李	lǐ
7	沒	méi
7	那	nà
7	男	nán

Pinyin	Character	Lesson		Stroke#	Character	Pinyin
guó	國	6		7	你	nǐ
guò	過	29		7	努	nǔ
hái	孩	14		7	判	pàn
hái	還	19		7	身	shēn
hàn	漢	6		7	束	shù
háng	行	14		7	忘	wàng
hǎo	好	1		7	位	wèi
hào	號	10		7	我	wǒ
hē	喝	8		7	吸	xī
hé	和	13		7	系	xì
hé	河	25		7	找	zhǎo
hè	賀	20		7	址	zhǐ
hěn	很	2		7	志	zhì
hóng	紅	19		7	住	zhù
hòu	後	17		7	助	zhù
hòu	候	18		7	走	zǒu
hù	互	15		7	足	zú
huā	花	19		7	作	zuò
huá	滑	28		7	坐	zuò
huà	畫	11		8	爸	bà
huà	話	23		8	杯	bēi
huà	化	27		8	表	biǎo
huān	歡	8		8	到	dào
huán	還	11		8	的	de
huí	回	17		8	典	diǎn
huì	會	20		8	店	diàn
huǒ	火	24		8	定	dìng
huò	或	26		8	東	dōng
jī	機	29		8	兒	ér
jǐ	幾	15		8	房	fáng

Pinyin	Character	Lesson		Stroke#	Character	Pinyin
jǐ	己	30		8	放	fàng
jiā	家	14		8	法	fǎ
jiā	加	20		8	非	fēi
jiān	間	22		8	服	fú
jiàn	見	11		8	姑	gū
jiàn	件	16		8	和	hé
jiàn	健	27		8	河	hé
jiào	教	15		8	花	huā
jiào	叫	9		8	或	huò
jiào	覺	18		8	姐	jiě
jiē	接	23		8	京	jīng
jiě	姐	14		8	咖	kā
jiě	解	26		8	刻	kè
jiè	介	13		8	空	kòng
jīn	今	20		8	來	lái
jǐn	緊	29		8	兩	liǎng
jìn	進	8		8	每	měi
jīng	京	16		8	妹	mèi
jìng	竟	26		8	門	mén
jiū	究	26		8	明	míng
jiǔ	九	11		8	呢	ne
jiǔ	酒	19		8	念	niàn
jiù	舊	16		8	朋	péng
jiù	就	26		8	衫	shān
jú	橘	19		8	舍	shě
jù	劇	16		8	始	shǐ
kā	咖	17		8	使	shǐ
kāi	開	21		8	事	shì
kàn	看	7		8	所	suǒ
kāng	康	27		8	玩	wàn

Pinyin	Character	Lesson		**Stroke#**	Character	Pinyin
kě	可	26		8	些	xiē
kè	客	8		8	姓	xìng
kè	刻	17		8	易	yì
kè	課	17		8	迎	yíng
kòng	空	20		8	泳	yǒng
kǒu	口	15		8	招	zhāo
kū	哭	30		8	者	zhě
kuài	快	25		8	知	zhí
kuài	筷	27		8	注	zhù
kuàng	礦	25		9	城	chéng
lái	來	13		9	待	dài
lǎn	覽	15		9	飛	fēi
lǎo	老	6		9	孩	hái
lào	酪	25		9	很	hěn
le	了	13		9	紅	hóng
lí	離	29		9	後	hòu
lǐ	理	22		9	看	kàn
lǐ	裏	22		9	客	kè
lǐ	李	28		9	亮	liang
lì	力	29		9	茅	mao
liǎ	倆	26		9	面	mian
liàn	煉	24		9	前	qian
liàn	練	24		9	秋	qiū
liǎng	兩	16		9	泉	quan
liang	亮	21		9	什	shen
líng	〇	10		9	食	shí
líng	零	10		9	是	shì
liu	留	9		9	室	shì
liu	六	11		9	思	sī
lou	樓	27		9	為	wèi

Pinyin	Character	Lesson
lu	路	29
lǜ	綠	16
ma	嗎	2
mā	媽	4
mǎi	買	13
man	慢	25
mang	忙	3
mao	茅	27
mao	帽	28
me	麼	7
mei	沒	14
měi	每	18
mèi	妹	14
men	們	3
men	門	21
mian	面	22
mian	麵	25
min	民	19
ming	名	13
ming	明	23
nǎ	哪	6
na	那	5
nǎi	奶	25
nan	男	13
nan	難	24
ne	呢	2
neng	能	26
nǐ	你	1
nian	年	20
nian	念	24

Stroke#	Character	Pinyin
9	臥	wo
9	洗	xǐ
9	相	xiāng
9	相	xiàng
9	信	xìn
9	星	xīng
9	要	yào
9	音	yīn
9	英	yīng
9	怎	zěn
9	祝	zhù
9	昨	zuó
10	班	bān
10	茶	chá
10	差	chà
10	穿	chuān
10	高	gāo
10	哥	gē
10	個	gè
10	候	hòu
10	家	jiā
10	酒	jiǔ
10	哭	kū
10	倆	liǎ
10	留	liu
10	們	men
10	哪	nǎ
10	能	neng
10	娘	niang
10	旁	pang

Pinyin	Character	Lesson		Stroke#	Character	Pinyin
niang	娘	21		10	起	qǐ
nín	您	8		10	氣	qì
nóng	農	24		10	容	róng
nǔ	努	29		10	師	shī
nǚ	女	12		10	時	shí
pàn	判	28		10	書	shū
páng	旁	22		10	送	sòng
péng	朋	4		10	條	tiáo
pí	啤	19		10	務	wù
piàn	片	23		10	息	xi
piào	票	16		10	夏	xià
piāo	漂	21		10	笑	xiào
píng	瓶	19		10	烟	yān
píng	平	28		10	員	yuán
pu	葡	27		10	院	yuàn
qī	七	11		10	站	zhàn
qí	期	20		10	真	zhēn
qǐ	起	17		10	紙	zhǐ
qì	氣	8		10	桌	zhuō
qiān	簽	28		11	啊	à
qián	前	25		11	參	cān
qīng	輕	21		11	常	cháng
qíng	情	30		11	唱	chàng
qǐng	請	8		11	從	cóng
qiū	秋	29		11	得	dé
qiú	球	28		11	釣	diào
qù	去	12		11	頂	dǐng
quán	泉	26		11	都	dōu
qún	裙	16		11	訪	fǎng
ràng	讓	19		11	啡	fēi

Pinyin	Character	Lesson		Stroke#	Character	Pinyin
rè	熱	30		11	乾	gān
rén	人	6		11	國	guó
rèn	認	12		11	健	jiàn
rì	日	20		11	教	jiao
róng	容	26		11	接	jiē
sài	賽	28		11	竟	jìng
sān	三	10		11	康	kāng
shān	衫	16		11	理	lǐ
shāng	商	13		11	您	nín
shàng	上	16		11	啤	pí
shǎo	少	10		11	票	piào
shào	紹	13		11	瓶	píng
shè	舍	10		11	情	qíng
shéi	誰	6		11	球	qiú
shēn	深	26		11	商	shāng
shēn	身	29		11	紹	shào
shén	甚	7		11	深	shēn
shén	什	7		11	視	shì
shēng	生	9		11	宿	sù
shī	師	6		11	堂	tang
shí	十	11		11	停	tíng
shí	食	17		11	晚	wǎn
shí	時	18		11	爲	wèi
shǐ	始	27		11	問	wèn
shǐ	使	27		11	習	xí
shì	是	4		11	現	xiàn
shì	識	12		11	研	yán
shì	室	15		11	魚	yú
shì	事	17		11	張	zhāng
shì	視	23		11	這	zhe

Pinyin	_Character_	_Lesson_	**Stroke#**	_Character_	_Pinyin_
shì	試	27	12	報	bào
shū	書	5	12	備	bèi
shū	輸	28	12	筆	bǐ
shù	束	21	12	裁	cái
shuāng	雙	28	12	菜	cài
shuǐ	水	19	12	場	chǎng
shuì	睡	18	12	詞	cí
shuō	說	13	12	答	dá
sī	思	20	12	等	děng
sì	四	10	12	隊	duì
sòng	送	21	12	發	fā
sù	宿	10	12	飯	fàn
sù	訴	14	12	復	fù
suì	歲	20	12	敢	gǎn
suǒ	所	29	12	給	gěi
tā	他	3	12	貴	guì
tā	她	5	12	喝	hē
tái	台	27	12	賀	hè
tài	太	16	12	畫	huà
tán	談	26	12	間	jiān
tāng	湯	25	12	進	jìn
táng	堂	17	12	幾	jǐ
tao	萄	27	12	就	jiù
tī	踢	28	12	開	kāi
tí	題	18	12	裏	lǐ
tǐ	體	29	12	嗎	ma
tiān	天	18	12	媽	mā
tiáo	條	16	12	買	mǎi
tiào	跳	21	12	帽	mào
tīng	聽	19	12	期	qī

Pinyin	Character	Lesson
tīng	廳	22
tíng	停	25
tong	同	20
tú	圖	7
tuan	團	23
tuǐ	腿	25
wài	外	9
wán	玩	23
wǎn	晚	16
wàng	忘	29
wèi	喂	13
wèi	位	25
wèi	為	27
wèi	爲	27
wen	文	15
wen	聞	23
wèn	問	9
wǒ	我	2
wò	臥	22
wǔ	五	10
wǔ	午	18
wǔ	舞	20
wù	務	19
xī	吸	8
xī	西	30
xí	習	9
xí	息	18
xǐ	喜	19
xǐ	洗	22
xì	系	15

Stroke#	Character	Pinyin
12	裙	qún
12	訴	sù
12	湯	tāng
12	萄	tao
12	喂	wèi
12	喜	xǐ
12	椅	yǐ
12	游	yóu
12	準	zhǔn
13	愛	ài
13	當	dāng
13	道	dào
13	電	diàn
13	該	gāi
13	感	gǎn
13	跟	gēn
13	過	guò
13	號	hào
13	滑	huá
13	話	huà
13	會	huì
13	解	jiě
13	筷	kuài
13	酪	lào
13	煉	liàn
13	零	líng
13	路	lù
13	農	nóng
13	葡	pú
13	試	shì

Pinyin	Character	Lesson	Stroke#	Character	Pinyin
xià	下	11	13	歲	suì
xià	夏	29	13	跳	tiào
xiān	先	12	13	想	xiǎng
xiàn	現	11	13	新	xīn
xiāng	相	15	13	煙	yān
xiāng	箱	28	13	意	yì
xiǎng	想	14	13	園	yuan
xiàng	相	21	13	照	zhao
xiàng	像	21	13	準	zhǔn
xiǎo	小	19	14	嘗	cháng
xiao	笑	30	14	對	duì
xiē	些	24	14	輔	fǔ
xie	鞋	28	14	歌	gē
xiě	寫	14	14	漢	hàn
xie	謝	8	14	慢	man
xīn	新	15	14	麼	me
xīn	心	24	14	漂	piào
xìn	信	14	14	輕	qīng
xīng	星	20	14	認	ren
xìng	姓	9	14	睡	shui
xìng	興	21	14	說	shuō
xiū	休	18	14	團	tuan
xué	學	9	14	腿	tuǐ
yān	煙	8	14	圖	tu
yān	烟	8	14	聞	wen
yan	研	26	14	像	xiàng
yang	樣	22	14	銀	yín
yào	要	19	14	語	yǔ
yě	也	2	14	遠	yuǎn
yī	一	10	14	誌	zhì

146

Pinyin	Character	Lesson	Stroke#	Character	Pinyin
yǐ	以	17	15	層	céng
yǐ	椅	22	15	廠	chǎng
yì	意	20	15	厨	chú
yì	譯	26	15	緊	jǐn
yì	易	26	15	劇	jù
yì	誼	27	15	課	kè
yīn	音	19	15	練	liàn
yín	銀	14	15	樓	lóu
yīng	英	12	15	綠	lǜ
yīng	應	26	15	請	qǐng
yíng	迎	8	15	熱	rè
yíng	贏	28	15	誰	shéi
yǐng	影	17	15	談	tán
yǒng	泳	25	15	踢	tī
yòng	用	11	15	舞	wǔ
yóu	游	25	15	箱	xiāng
yǒu	友	4	15	鞋	xié
yǒu	有	14	15	寫	xiě
yòu	又	27	15	樣	yàng
yú	魚	25	15	誼	yì
yǔ	語	6	15	影	yǐng
yuán	員	19	15	閱	yuè
yuán	園	22	15	樂	yuè
yuǎn	遠	30	16	辦	bàn
yuàn	院	9	16	餐	cān
yuàn	願	29	16	錯	cuò
yuè	閱	15	16	導	dǎo
yuè	樂	19	16	懂	dǒng
yuè	月	20	16	館	guǎn
zá	雜	15	16	機	jī

Pinyin	Character	Lesson		Stroke#	Character	Pinyin
zài	在	10		16	橘	jú
zài	再	11		16	輸	shū
zàn	贊	27		16	興	xìng
zǎo	澡	22		16	學	xué
zǎo	早	26		16	澡	zǎo
zěn	怎	22		16	整	zhěng
zhàn	站	29		17	幫	bāng
zhāng	張	16		17	點	diǎn
zhāo	招	27		17	鍛	duàn
zhǎo	找	16		17	還	huán
zhao	照	23		17	賽	sài
zhě	者	26		17	謝	xiè
zhe	這	4		17	應	yìng
zhēn	真	21		17	總	zǒng
zhěng	整	22		18	邊	biān
zheng	正	23		18	翻	fān
zheng	證	28		18	舊	jiù
zhī	知	20		18	雙	shuāng
zhǐ	紙	13		18	題	tí
zhǐ	址	20		18	雜	za
zhì	誌	15		19	礦	kuàng
zhì	志	26		19	離	lí
zhōng	中	15		19	難	nan
zhù	住	10		19	簽	qiān
zhù	祝	20		19	識	shì
zhù	助	22		19	願	yuàn
zhù	注	29		19	贊	zàn
zhǔn	準	25		19	證	zhèng
zhǔn	準	25		20	覺	jiào
zhuō	桌	22		20	麵	mian

148

Pinyin	Character	Lesson
zǐ	子	14
zì	字	13
zì	自	30
zǒng	總	22
zǒu	走	17
zu	足	28
zuó	昨	28
zuǒ	左	22
zuò	坐	10
zuò	作	14

Stroke#	Character	Pinyin
20	譯	yì
20	贏	yíng
21	襯	chèn
22	歡	huān
22	覽	lǎn
22	聽	tīng
23	體	tǐ
24	讓	ràng
25	觀	guān
25	廳	tīng

Character Conversion Table

Lesson	2	3	4		5		6			
Simplified	吗	们	这	妈	车	书	国	谁	师	汉
Traditional	嗎	們	這	媽	車	書	國	誰	師	漢

Lesson	6	7			8					9
Simplified	语	什	么	图	请	进	欢	谢	气	贵
Traditional	語	甚	麼	圖	請	進	歡	謝	氣	貴

Lesson	9			10			11			
Simplified	问	学	习	儿	号	层	还	画	报	词
Traditional	問	學	習	兒	號	層	還	畫	報	詞

Lesson	11		12		13					
Simplified	现	见	认	识	英	买	笔	纸	来	绍
Traditional	現	見	認	識	英	買	筆	紙	來	紹

Lesson	13	14							15	
Simplified	对	说	银	爱	给	写	诉	个	几	当
Traditional	對	說	銀	愛	給	寫	訴	個	幾	當

Lesson	15					16			
Simplified	阅	览	杂	志	馆	条	两	张	剧	从
Traditional	閱	覽	雜	誌	館	條	兩	張	劇	從

Lesson	16		17				18		
Simplified	旧	衬	绿	点	课	后	电	饭	时	题
Traditional	舊	襯	綠	點	課	後	電	飯	時	題

Lesson	18	19							20
Simplified	觉	务	员	红	桔	听	乐	让	辅	导
Traditional	覺	務	員	紅	橘	聽	樂	讓	輔	導

Lesson	20				21			22	
Simplified	岁	贺	会	参	兴	轻	开	门	边	园
Traditional	歲	賀	會	參	興	輕	開	門	邊	園

Lesson	22						23		
Simplified	厅	总	帮	里	间	样	视	话	复	闻
Traditional	廳	總	幫	裏	間	樣	視	話	復	聞

Lesson	23				24				
Simplified	团	观	厂	访	发	农	锻	炼	难	练
Traditional	團	觀	廠	訪	發	農	鍛	煉	難	練

Lesson	25								26
Simplified	准	备	钓	鱼	汤	错	面	矿	研	谈
Traditional	準	備	釣	魚	湯	錯	麵	礦	研	談

Lesson	26				27				
Simplified	译	应	该	俩	尝	为	干	谊	试	赞
Traditional	譯	應	該	倆	嘗	爲	乾	誼	試	贊

Lesson	27	28							
Simplified	楼	赛	办	签	证	队	赢	输	顶	双
Traditional	樓	賽	辦	簽	證	隊	贏	輸	頂	雙

Lesson	29								30
Simplified	飞	机	场	愿	离	紧	体	过	东	热
Traditional	飛	機	場	願	離	緊	體	過	東	熱

Lesson	30								
Simplified	远
Traditional	遠

PCR I Vocabulary

Lesson Sequence

Lesson	Pinyin	Characters	Function	English meaning
1	hǎo	好	adj, v-state	good, to be good, to be well
1	nǐ	你	pron	you
1*	Gǔbō	古波	n-prop	Gubo
1*	Pàlánkǎ	帕蘭卡	prop	Palanka
2	hěn	很	adv	very
2	ma	嗎	particle	an interrogative particle
2	ne	呢	particle	a modal particle
2	wǒ	我	pron	I, me
2	yě	也	adv	also, too
3	bù	不	adv	not, no
3	dìdi	弟弟	n	younger brother
3	dōu	都	adv	all
3	gēge	哥哥	n	elder brother
3	máng	忙	adj. v-state	busy, to be busy
3	tā	他	pron	he, him
3	tāmen	們	pron	they, them
4	bàba	爸爸	n	father
4	māma	媽媽	n	mother
4	nǐmen	你們	pron	you (pl.)
4	péngyou	朋友	n	friend

Note: * = Proper Noun
            ** = Supplementary word

153

Lesson	Pinyin	Characters	Function	English meaning
4	zhè	這	pron	this
5	chē	車	n	car
5	dàifu	大夫	n	doctor
5	de	的	particle	a structural particle
5	nà	那	pron	that
5	shū	書	n	book
5	tā	她	pron	she, her
5**	bào	報	n	newspaper
5**	bǐ	筆	n	pen, pencil, brush-pen
5**	chǐ	尺	n	ruler
5**	zhǐ	紙	n	paper
6	guó	國	n	country, state
6	Hànyǔ	漢語	n	Chinese (language)
6	lǎo	老	adj., v-state	old, to be old
6	lǎoshī	老師	n	teacher
6	nǎ	哪	pron	which
6	rén	人	n	person
6	shéi	誰	pron	who
6	wǒmen	我們	pron	we, us
6*	Zhōngguó	中國	n-prop	China
6**	Déguó	德國	n-prop	Germany
6**	Fǎguó	法國	n-prop	France
6**	Mǎlǐ	馬里	n-prop	Mali
6**	Měiguó	美國	n-prop	U.S.A.
6**	Rìběn	日本	n-prop	Japan
7	dìtú	地圖	n	map, atlas
7	kàn	看	v-act	to look, to read, to watch
7	shénme	甚麼	pron	what
7*	Běijīng	北京	n-prop	Beijing
7*	Chángjiāng	長江	n-prop	The Yangtze River
7*	Huáng Hé	黃河	n-prop	The Yellow River

Lesson	Pinyin	Characters	Function	English meaning
7*	Shànghǎi	上海	n-prop	Shanghai
7*	Chángchéng	長城	n-prop	The Great Wall
7**	Dàyáng Zhōu	大洋洲	n-prop	Oceania
7**	Fēi Zhōu	非洲	n-prop	Africa
7**	Nán Měi Zhōu	南美洲	n-prop	South America
7**	Ōu Zhōu	歐洲	n-prop	Europe
7**	shìjiè	世界	n	world
8	chá	茶	n	tea
8	hē	喝	v-act	to drink
8	huānyíng	歡迎	v-act	to welcome
8	jìn	進	v-act	to enter, to come in
8	kèqi	客氣	adj, v-state	polite, to be polite
8	nín	您	pron	polite form of "nǐ"
8	qǐng	請	v-act	please
8	xī yān	吸煙 (烟)	v-act	to smoke
8	yān	煙 (烟)	n	cigarette
8	xièxie	謝謝	v-act	to thank
8*	Wáng	王	n-prop	Wang
8**	kāfēi	咖啡	n	coffee
8**	niúnǎi	牛奶	n	milk
8**	píjiǔ	啤酒	n	beer
8**	tàitai	太太	n	Mrs., madame
8**	xiānsheng	先生	n	Mr., sir, gentleman
9	guì xìng	貴姓	idiom	What's your name?
9	jiào	叫	v-id	to call, to be called
9	liúxuéshēng	留學生	n	a foreign student
9	qǐngwèn	請問	idiom	May I ask...?
9	wàiyǔ	外語	n	foreign language
9	wèn	問	v-act	to ask
9	xìng	姓	n, v-id	a surname, (one's) surname is...
9	xué	學	v	to study, to learn

Lesson	Pinyin	Characters	Function	English meaning
9	xuésheng	學生	n	student
9	xuéxí	學習	v	to study, to learn
9	xuéyuàn	學院	n	college, institute
9*	Dīng Yún	丁雲	n-prop	Ding Yun
9**	Cháoxiǎn	朝鮮	n-prop	Korea
9**	nǚshì	女士	n	polite address to a lady
9**	tóngzhì	同志	n	comrade
9**	xiǎojie	小姐	n	miss
9**	Yīngguó	英國	n-prop	Britain
10	céng	層	measure	story (of a building)
10	duōshao	多少	pron	how many, how much
10	èr	二	number	two
10	hào	號	n	number
10	líng	零	number	zero
10	nǎr	哪兒	pron	where
10	sān	三	number	three
10	sì	四	number	four
10	sùshè	宿舍	n	dormitory
10	wǔ	五	number	five
10	yī	一	number	one
10	zài	在	v-loc	to be at, to be in
10	zhù	住	v-loc	to live
10	zuò	坐	v-act	to sit, to take a seat
10**	cèsuǒ	廁所	n	toilet, lavatory
10**	nàr	那兒	pron	there
10**	yīyuàn	醫院	n	hospital
10**	zhèr	這兒	pron	here
11	bā	八	number	eight
11	cídiǎn	詞典	n	dictionary
11	huàbào	畫報	n	pictorial

156

Lesson	Pinyin	Characters	Function	English meaning
11	huán	還	v-act	to return
11	jiǔ	九	number	nine
11	liù	六	number	six
11	qī	七	number	seven
11	shí	十	number	ten
11	xiànzài	現在	n-time	now, nowadays
11	yíxiàr	一下兒	idiom	a little while
11	yòng	用	v-act	to use, to make use of
11	zàijiàn	再見	idiom	See you again; Good bye
11**	běnzi	本子	n	note-book
11**	diànhuà	電話	n	telephone, telephone call
11**	yǔsǎn	雨傘	n	umbrella
11**	zázhì	雜誌	n	magazine
12	cháng	常	adv	often
12	Fǎyǔ	法語	n	French
12	nǔ	女	adj	female
12	qù	去	v-act	to go
12	rènshi	認識	v-cog	to know, to recognize
12	tāmen	她們	pron	they, them (for females)
12	xiānsheng	先生	n	Mr., sir, gentleman
12	Yīngyǔ	英語	n	English
13	a	啊	interj	oh
13	bǐ	筆	n	pen
13	duì	對	v-state	to be right, to be correct
13	hé	和	conj	and, with
13	jièshào	介紹	v-act	to introduce
13	lái	來	v-act	to come
13	le	了	particle	a modal particle
13	mǎi	買	v-act	to buy
13	míngzi	名	n	name
13	nán	男	adj	male

Lesson	Pinyin	Characters	Function	English meaning
13	shāngdiàn	商店	n	shop
13	shuō	說	v-act	to speak, to say
13	wèi	喂	interj	hello
13	zhǐ	紙	n	paper
13*	Dīng Yún	丁雲	n-prop	Ding Yun
13*	Gǔbō	古波	n-prop	Gubo
13*	Pàlánkǎ	帕蘭卡	n-prop	Palanka
13*	Zhōngguó	中國	n-prop	China
13**	běnzi	本子	n	note-book
13**	Fǎguó	法國	n-prop	France
13**	jiàoshòu	教授	n	professor
13**	Yīngguó	英國	n-prop	Britain
13**	yóujú	郵局	n	post office
13**	yóupiào	郵票	n	stamp
14	àiren	愛人	n	spouse
14	gàosu	告訴	v-act	to tell
14	gěi	給	co-v, v-act	to, for, to give
14	gōngzuò	工作	n, v-act	work, to work
14	háizi	孩子	n	child
14	jiā	家	n	family, home, house
14	jiějie	姐姐	n	elder sister
14	méi	沒	adv, v-poss	not, no, do not have
14	mèimei	妹妹	n	younger sister
14	shūdiàn	書店	n	bookstore
14	xiǎng	想	v-act, v-int	to think, to miss, to want
14	xiě	寫	v-act	to write
14	xìn	信	n	letter
14	yínháng	銀行	n	bank
14	yǒu	有	v-poss	to have, there be
14	zuò	作	v-act	to do
14**	gōngchéngshī	工程師	n	engineer

Lesson	Pinyin	Characters	Function	English meaning
14**	gōngsī	公司	n	company
14**	jīnglǐ	經理	n	manager, director
14**	zhíyuán	職員	n	office worker, staff
15	bào	報	n	newspaper
15	běn	本	measure	volume
15	bù gǎndāng	不敢當	idiom	I don't really deserve it.
15	ge	個	measure	a measure word
15	hái	還	adv	still, in addition, else
15	Hànzì	漢字	n	Chinese character
15	hùxiāng	互相	adv	each other, mutually
15	jǐ	幾	pron/numb.	how many, how much, several
15	jiāo	教	v-act	to teach
15	kǒuyǔ	口語	n	spoken language
15	nàr	那兒	pron	there
15	túshūguǎn	圖書館	n	library
15	xì	系	n	department, faculty
15	xīn	新	adj, v-state	new, to be new
15	yǔfǎ	語法	n	grammar
15	yuèlǎnshì	閱覽室	n	reading room
15	zázhì	雜誌	n	magazine
15	Zhōngwén	中文	n	Chinese (language)
15	zì	字	n	character
15*	Wáng	王	n-prop	Wang
15**	bān	班	n	class, squad
15**	jiàoshì	教室	n	classroom
15**	jiè	借	v-act	to borrow, to lend
15**	shēngcí	生詞	n	new word
15**	shíyànshì	實驗室	n	laboratory
16	bái	白	adj, v-state	white, to be white
16	chènshān	襯衫	n	shirt, blouse
16	chuān	穿	v-act	to put on, to wear

Lesson	Pinyin	Characters	Function	English meaning
16	cóng	從	co-v	from
16	dà	大	adj, v-state	big, large, to be big, to be large
16	jiàn	件	measure	a measure word
16	jīngjù	京劇	n	Beijing opera
16	jiù	舊	adj, v-state	old, to be old
16	liǎng	兩	number	two
16	lǜ	綠	adj, v-state	green, to be green
16	piào	票	n	ticket
16	qúnzi	裙子	n	skirt
16	tài	太	adv	too, too much
16	tiáo	條	measure	a measure word
16	wǎnshang	晚上	n	evening
16	zhāng	張	measure	piece
16	zhǎo	找	v-act	to look for, to call on (a person)
16	zhèr	這兒	pron	here
16**	dàyī	大衣	n	overcoat, topcoat
16**	hēi	黑	adj, v-state	black, to be black
16**	jùchǎng	劇場	n	theatre
16**	kùzi	褲子	n	trousers
16**	lán	藍	adj, v-state	blue, to be blue
16**	shàngyī	上衣	n	upper outer garment
16**	zuòwèi	座位	n	seat
17	a	啊	particle	Ah, (a modal particle)
17	bàn	半	number	half
17	chà	差	v-state	to be short of, to lack
17	kāfēiguǎn	咖啡館	n	café
17	děng	等	v-act	to wait
17	diǎn	點	measure	o'clock, point
17	diànyǐng	電影	n	film, movie
17	fēn	分	measure	minute
17	gēn	跟	co-v, v	with, to follow

Lesson	Pinyin	Characters	Function	English meaning
17	huí	回	v-act	to return
17	kāfēi	咖啡	n	coffee
17	kè	刻	measure	quarter (or an hour)
17	kè	課	n	class
17	lù	路	n	road, way
17	shàng(kè)	上課	v-act	to attend or to teach (a class)
17	shítáng	食堂	n	dining-hall
17	shìr	事兒	n	business, thing
17	xià(kè)	下課	v-act	class is over or dismissed
17	yǐhòu	以後	n	later on, in the future
17	yìqǐ	一起	adv	together
17	zǒu	走	v-act	to go, to walk
17**	biǎo	錶	n	watch
17**	diànyǐngyuàn	電影院	n	cinema
17**	shàng bān	上班	idiom	to go to work
17**	xià bān	下班	idiom	to come or go off work
17**	yǐqián	以前	n-time	before, in the past, ago
17**	zhōng	鐘	n	clock
18	chī	吃	v-act	to eat
18	chuáng	床	n	bed
18	duō	多	adj, v-state	many, much, a lot of
18	fàn	飯	n	meal, cooked rice, food
18	měi	每	pron	every, each
18	qǐ	起	v-act	to get up, to rise
18	qǐ chuáng	起床	idiom	to get up
18	shàngwǔ	上午	n-time	morning
18	shuì jiào	睡覺	idiom	to go to bed, to sleep
18	tiān	天	n	day
18	wèntí	問題	n	question
18	xiàwǔ	下午	n-time	afternoon
18	xiūxi	休息	v-act	to take a rest

Lesson	Pinyin	Characters	Function	English meaning
18	yǒu shíhou	有時候	idiom	sometimes
18*	Běijīng	北京	n-prop	Beijing
19	bēi	杯	measure	cup
19	bié	別	adv	don't
19	chàng	唱	v-act	to sing
19	fúwùyuán	服務員	n	waiter, waitress, attendant
19	gēr	歌兒	n	song
19	gǔdiǎn	古典	n	classical, classic
19	háishì	還是	conj	or
19	hóng	紅	adj, v-state	red, to be red
19	hóngchá	紅茶	n	black tea
19	huāchá	花茶	n	scented tea, jasmine tea
19	júzi	橘子	n	orange
19	júzishuǐ	橘子水	n	orangeade, orange juice
19	míngē	民歌	n	folk song
19	píjiǔ	啤酒	n	beer
19	píng	瓶	measure	bottle
19	ràng	讓	v-act	to let, to ask
19	shuǐ	水	n	water
19	tīng	聽	v-act	to listen
19	xǐhuan	喜歡	v-act	to like, to be fond of
19	xiàndài	現代	n	modern
19	xiǎojie	小姐	n	miss, young lady
19	yào	要	v-int, v-act	must, to be going to, to want
19	yīnyuè	音樂	n	music
19**	chàngpiàn	唱片	n	gramophone record
19**	lǜchá	綠茶	n	green tea
19**	píngguǒ	蘋果	n	apple
19**	pútao	葡萄	n	grape
19**	táng	糖	n	sugar, sweets, candy
19**	xiāngjiāo	香蕉	n	banana

Lesson	Pinyin	Characters	Function	English meaning
19**	zhī	枝	measure	branch, etc.
20	bān	班	n	class, squad
20	cānjiā	參加	v-act	to take part in, to attend
20	dìzhǐ	地址	n	address
20	fǔdǎo	輔導	v-act	to coach
20	hào	號	n	date, day of the month
20	jīnnián	今年	n	this year
20	jīntiān	今天	n	today
20	kòngr	空兒	n	spare time
20	nián	年	n	year
20	rì	日	n	date, day of the month
20	shēngri	生日	n	birthday
20	suì	歲	measure	year (age)
20	tóngxué	同學	n	classmate, schoolmate
20	wǔhuì	舞會	n	dance, ball
20	xīngqī	星期	n	week
20	xīngqīrì	星期日	n	Sunday
20	yídìng	一定	adj, adv	particular, surely, certainly
20	yǒu yìsi	有意思	adj-comb	interesting
20	yuè	月	n	month
20	zhīdao	知道	v-cog	to know
20	zhùhè	祝賀	n, v-act	congratulation, to congratulate
20**	duì bu qǐ	對不起	idiom	I'm sorry
20**	jié hūn	結婚	v-comb	to get married
20**	méi guānxi	沒關係	idiom	it doesn't matter
20**	míngnián	明年	n	next year
20**	qùnián	去年	n	last year
20**	tán	談	v-act	to talk, to chat
20**	yīnyuèhuì	音樂會	n	concert
20**	yuēhuì	約會	n	appointment

Lesson	Pinyin	Characters	Function	English meaning
21	ba	吧	particle	(a modal particle)
21	duō	多	adv	how
21	fēicháng	非常	adv	extremely
21	gǎnxie	感謝	v-act	to thank
21	gāoxìng	高興	adj, v-state	happy, to be glad, to be delighted
21	gèng	更	adv	even, still
21	gūniang	姑娘	n	girl
21	hǎokàn	好看	adj, v-state	good-looking, to be pretty
21	huār	花兒	n	flower
21	kāi	開	v-act	to open
21	mén	門	n	door
21	niánqīng	年輕	adj, v-state	young, to be young
21	piàoliang	漂亮	adj. v-state	pretty, to be pretty, (to be) beautiful
21	shù	束	measure	bunch
21	sòng	送	v-act	to give, to give as a present
21	tàitai	太太	n	Mrs., madame
21	tiào wǔ	跳舞	v-comb	to dance
21	xiàng	像	v-id	to be like, to resemble
21	zhēn	真	adj	real, true, genuine
21	zhù	祝	v-act	to wish
21*	Bùlǎng	布朗	n-prop	Brown, a personal name
21*	Rìběn	日本	n-prop	Japan
21**	érzi	兒子	n	son
21**	gānjìng	乾净	adj, v-state	clean, neat, to be clean, to be neat
21**	lǐwù	禮物	n	present, gift
21**	liàng	輛	measure	measure word for vehicle
21**	nǚér	女兒	n	daughter
21**	suìshu	歲數	n	age
21**	xīnnián	新年	n	New Year
21**	zhàopiàn	照片	n	photograph, picture

Lesson	Pinyin	Characters	Function	English meaning
22	bāng	幫	v-act	to help
22	bāngzhu	幫助	n, v-act	help, to help
22	cāntīng	餐廳	n	dining-hall
22	chúfáng	厨房	n	kitchen
22	duìmiàn	對面	n	opposite
22	fángjiān	房間	n	room
22	fángzi	房子	n	house
22	hòubiān	後邊	n	back, at the back of, behind
22	huāyuán	花園	n	garden
22	kètīng	客廳	n	drawing room, parlour
22	lǐbiān	裏邊	n	inside
22	pángbiān	旁邊	n	side
22	shàngbiān	上邊	n	top, on, over, above
22	shǎo	少	adj, v-state	few, little, to be few, to be little
22	shūfáng	書房	n	study
22	wòshì	卧室	n	bedroom
22	xǐ zǎo	洗澡	v-act	to take a bath
22	xǐzǎojiān	洗澡間	n	bathroom
22	xiǎo	小	adj, v-state	little, small, to be little, to be small
22	yǐzi	椅子	n	chair
22	zěnmeyàng	怎麼樣	idiom	how is it
22	zhěnglǐ	整理	v-act	to put in order, to straighten up
22	zhuōzi	桌子	n	table
22	zǒng	總	adv	always
22	zǒngshì	總是	adv	always
22	zuǒbiān	左邊	n	left
22**	bǎ	把	measure	measure word
22**	chuānghu	窗户	n	window
22**	qiánbiān	前邊	n	front, in front of, before
22**	tào	套	measure	set
22**	wàibiān	外邊	n	outside

Lesson	Pinyin	Characters	Function	English meaning
22**	xiàbiān	下邊	n	bottom
22**	yòubiān	右邊	n	right
22**	zhōngjiān	中間	n	middle
23	cānguān	參觀	v-act	to visit, to pay a visit
23	chéng	城	n	city, town
23	chūfā	出發	v-act	to start out, to set off
23	dǎ (diànhuà)	打(電話)	v-act	to make (a telephone call)
23	dàibiǎo	代表	n	delegate, representative
23	dàibiǎotuán	代表團	n	delegation
23	diànhuà	電話	n	telephone, telephone call
23	diànshì	電視	n	television
23	fǎngwèn	訪問	v-act	to visit, to call on
23	fùxí	復習	v-act	to review
23	gōngchǎng	工廠	n	factory
23	gōngrén	工人	n	worker
23	yǒuhǎo	友好	v-state	to be friendly
23	jiē (diànhuà)	接(電話)	v-act	to answer (the phone)
23	jiē (rén)	接(人)	ve-act	to meet (a person)
23	kāi (chē)	開(車)	v-act	to drive (a car)
23	kèwén	課文	n	text
23	méi (you)	沒(有)	adv	not, no
23	míngtiān	明天	n	tomorrow
23	wàibiān	外邊	n	outside
23	wánr	玩兒	v-act	to play, to have fun with
23	xīnwén	新聞	n	news
23	yǒuhǎo	友好	adj	friendly
23	zhàopiàn	照片	n	photograph, photo, picture
23	zhèngzài	正在	adv	(action in progress)
23*	Rénmín Rìbào	人民日報	n-prop	The People's Daily
23**	dǎ cuò le	打錯了	idiom	you (or I)'ve dialled the wrong #

Lesson	Pinyin	Characters	Function	English meaning
23**	fēnjī	分機	n	extension
23**	hàomǎ	號碼	n	number
23**	zhàn xiàn	佔綫	idiom	the line is busy
23**	zǒngjī	總機	n	central exchange, switchboard
24	cí	詞	n	word
24	diǎnxin	點心	n	light refreshments, pastry
24	dǒng	懂	v-cog	to understand
24	duànliàn	鍛煉	v-act	to do physical training
24	huídá	回答	v-act	to reply, to answer
24	huǒchē	火車	n	train
24	liànxí	練習	n, v-act	exercise, to practice
24	nán	難	adj, v-state	difficult, to be difficult
24	niàn	念	v-act	to read (aloud), to study
24	nóngcūn	農村	n	countryside, rural areas
24	nóngmín	農民	n	peasant
24	rènzhēn	認真	adj, v-state	(to be) conscientious /serious
24	shēngcí	生詞	n	new word
24	xiē	些	m	some
24*	Ānnà	安娜	n-prop	Anna
24*	Wáng Shūwén	王書文	n-prop	Wang Shuwen
25	búcuò	不錯	adj	correct, not bad, pretty good
25	de	得	particle	particle, structural
25	diào	釣	v-act	to fish with a hook and bait
25	hé	河	n	river
25	huǒtuǐ	火腿	n	ham
25	jiàoliàn	教練	n	coach, trainer
25	kuài	快	adj	fast, quick
25	kuàngquánshuǐ	礦泉水	n	mineral water
25	màn	慢	adj	slow
25	miànbāo	麵包	n	bread
25	nǎli	哪裏	idiom	it is nothing

Lesson	Pinyin	Characters	Function	English meaning
25	nǎilào	奶酪	n	cheese
25	qiánbiān	前邊	n	front
25	tāng	湯	n	soup
25	tíng	停	v-act	to stop, to come to a stop
25	wǎn	晚	adj	late
25	wèi	位	measure	measure word
25	yìdiǎnr	一點兒	idiom	a little, a bit
25	yóuyǒng	游泳	v-comb	to swim, swimming
25	yú	魚	n	fish
25	zài	再	adv	again, once more
25	zhǔnbèi	準備	v-act	to prepare
25**	bǐjiào	比較	adv, v-act	comparatively, to compare
25**	cài	菜	n	dish
25**	jīdàn	鷄蛋	n	hen's egg
25**	jiǎozi	餃子	n	Chinese dumpling
25**	liúlì	流利	adj	fluent
25**	niúnǎi	牛奶	n	milk (cows)
25**	qīngchu	清楚	adj	clear, distinct
25**	zhěngqí	整齊	adj, v-state	tidy, to be tidy
26	chéngyǔ	成語	n	proverb, idiom
26	dāng	當	v-id	to act as, to serve as
26	fānyì	翻譯	n, v-act	interpreter, to interpret / translate
26	huì	會	v-cog	to know how to, can
26	huòzhě	或者	conj	or
26	jiāshēn	加深	v-act	to deepen
26	jiù	就	adv, conj	at once, right away, then
26	kěshì	可是	conj	but
26	kěyǐ	可以	aux. v	may
26	lǐxiǎng	理想	n, adj	ideal
26	liǎ	倆	m	both, two
26	liǎojiě	了解	v-cog	to understand, to know

Lesson	Pinyin	Characters	Function	English meaning
26	néng	能	v-cog	can, to be able to
26	rénmín	人民	n	people
26	róngyi	容易	adj	easy
26	tán	談	v-act	to talk, to chat
26	wénxué	文學	n	literature
26	yánjiū	研究	n, v-act	research, to research, to study
26	yīnggāi	應該	?aux. v	should, ought to
26	yǒumíng	有名	adj	famous, well-known
26	zǎo	早	adj	early
26	zuòjiā	作家	n	writer
26*	Guō Mòruò	郭沫若	n-prop	Guo Moruo
26*	Lǔ Xùn	魯迅	n-prop	Lu Xun
26**	gējù	歌劇	n	opera
26**	huà	畫	v-act	to paint, to draw
26**	huàr	畫兒	n	painting, drawing, picture
26**	jìn lái	進來	v-comb	to come in, to enter
26**	shīgē	詩歌	n	poem
26**	wǎnfàn	晚飯	n	supper, dinner
26**	xiǎoshuō	小説	n	novel
27	cài	菜	n	dish, vegetable
27	cānzàn	參贊	n	counselor
27	cháng	嘗	v-act	to taste
27	dàjiā	大家	pron	all, everybody
27	dàshǐ	大使	n	ambassador
27	dàshǐguǎn	大使館	n	embassy
27	dào	到	v-act	to go, to arrive, to reach
27	fūren	夫人	n	lady, madame, Mrs.
27	gān bēi	乾杯	idiom	to propose a toast, here's to...
27	jiànkāng	健康	n, adj, v-st	health, healthy, to be healthy
27	jiǔ	酒	n	wine
27	kāishǐ	開始	v-act	to begin, to start

Lesson	Pinyin	Characters	Function	English meaning
27	kuàizi	筷子	n	chopsticks
27	lóu	樓	n	storied building, floor
27	máotáijiǔ	茅台酒	n	Maotai (a Chinese strong liquor)
27	pútao	葡萄	n	grape
27	pútaojiǔ	葡萄酒	n	grape wine
27	shì	試	v-act	to try
27	wèi	爲	prep	for, to
27	wénhuà	文化	n	culture
27	yǒuyì	友誼	n	friendship
27	yòu	又	adv	again, in addition to, more
27	zhāodàihuì	招待會	n	reception
27*	Lǐ	李	n-prop	Li
27**	bìng	病	n, ajd, v-st	illness, disease, sick, to fall ill
27**	báilándì	白蘭地	n	brandy
27**	wǔguān	武官	n	military attaché
27**	xiāngbīnjiǔ	香檳酒	n	champagne
27**	xiǎoxuéshēng	小學生	n	pupil, schoolboy/girl
27**	yīmì	一秘	n	first secretary
28	bàn	辦	v-act	to handle, to attend, to do
28	bǐ	比	prep, v-act	comparing to..., than, to compare
28	bīngxié	冰鞋	n	skating boots, skates
28	cáipàn	裁判	n, v-act	referee, umpire, to act as a referee
28	dǐng	頂	m	measure word for hat
28	dōngtiān	冬天	n	winter
28	duì	隊	n	team
28	gōngpíng	公平	adj	fair
28	huábīng	滑冰	v-comb	to skate, skating
28	màozi	帽子	n	hat, cap
28	qì rén	氣人	idiom	to get someone angry/annoyed
28	qiānzhèng	簽證	n	visa
28	qiú	球	n	ball

Lesson	Pinyin	Characters	Function	English meaning
28	sài	賽	n, v-act	competition, match, to compete
28	shū	輸	v-act	to lose
28	shuāng	雙	m	pair
28	tī	踢	v-act	to kick
28	wǔfàn	午飯	n	lunch
28	xiāngzi	箱子	n	suitcase
28	xié	鞋	n	shoes
28	xíngli	行李	n	luggage, baggage
28	yíng	贏	v-act	to beat, to win
28	zǎofàn	早飯	n	breakfast
28	zúqiú	足球	n	football
28	zuótiān	昨天	n	yesterday
28**	gōngyuán	公園	n	park
28**	huá xuě	滑雪	v-comb	to ski, skiing
28**	lánqiú	籃球	n	basketball
28**	páiqiú	排球	n	volleyball
28**	pīngpāngqiú	乒乓球	n	table tennis
28**	tǐyùchǎng	體育場	n	stadium
28**	yùndòng	運動	n, v-act	sports, to exercise, to work out
28**	wǎngqiú	網球	n	tennis
29	fàng xīn	放心	idiom	to set one's mind at rest
29	fēijī	飛機	n	aeroplane, plane, aircraft
29	fēnbié	分別	v-act	to part
29	jīchǎng	機場	n	airfield, airport
29	jiàn	見	v-act	to meet, to see
29	jiàn miàn	見面	v-comb	to meet (to see) each other
29	jǐn	緊	adj	close, tight, taut
29	jìnbù	進步	n, v-act	(to) advance, (to)progress
29	líkāi	離開	v-act	to leave
29	míngnián	明年	n	next year
29	nánguò	難過	adj	sad

Lesson	Pinyin	Characters	Function	English meaning
29	nǔlì	努力	adj	hard-working, studious
29	qǐfēi	起飛	v-act	to take off
29	qiūtiān	秋天	n	autumn
29	shàng	上	v-act	to get on, to get into, to board
29	shēntǐ	身體	n	body, health
29	suǒyǐ	所以	conj	so, therefore, as a result
29	wàng	忘	v-act	to forget
29	xiàtiān	夏天	n	summer
29	yào	要	adv	will, to be going to
29	yílùpíng'ān	一路平安	idiom	to have a pleasant journey
29	yuànyì	願意	v-int	to be willing
29	zhàn	站	v-act	to stand
29	zhào xiàng	照像(相)	v-comb	to take a picture
29	zhùyì	注意	v-act	to pay attention to
29**	chuán	船	n	ship
29**	jiào	叫	v-act	to hire, to call (a taxi, etc.)
29**	qìchē	汽車	n	car, vehicle
29**	sòngxíng	送行	v-act	to see someone off
29**	lǚxíng	旅行	v-act	to travel, to tour
29**	Zhōngguó Mínháng	中國民航	n-prop	CAAC
30	dōngxi	東西	n	thing
30	guójiā	國家	n	country
30	guò	過	v-act	to live, to get along
30	kū	哭	v	to cry, to weep
30	lí	離	prep	from
30	nǚ ér	女兒	n	daughter
30	qùnián	去年	n	last year
30	rèqíng	熱情	adj	cordial, enthusiastic
30	sòng (rén)	送(人)	v-act	to see (someone) off
30	xiào	笑	v-act	to laugh, to smile

Lesson	Pinyin	Characters	Function	English meaning
30	xīn	心	n	heart
30	yuǎn	遠	adj	far, distant
30	zìjǐ	自己	pron	self

PCR I Vocabulary

Pinyin Sequence

Pinyin	Characters	Functions	English meaning	Lesson
a	啊	particle	(a modal particle)	17
à	啊	interj	oh	13
àiren	愛人	n	spouse	14
Ānnà	安娜	n-prop	Anna	24*
ba	吧	particle	(a modal particle)	21
bā	八	number	eight	11
bǎ	把	measure	(a measure word)	22**
bàba	爸爸	n	father	4
bái	白	adj, v-state	white, to be write	16
báilándì	白蘭地	n	brandy	27**
bān	班	n	class, squad	15**, 20
bàn	辦	v-act	to handle, to attend, to do	28
bàn	半	number	half	17
bāng	幫	v-act	to help	22
bāngzhu	幫助	n, v-act	help, to help	22
bào	報	n	newspaper	5**, 15
bēi	杯	measure	cup	19
Běijīng	北京	n-prop	Beijing	7*, 18*
běn	本	measure	volume	15
běnzi	本子	n	note-book	11**,13**
bǐ	比	prep, v-act	than, to compare	28

Note: The Pinyin list follows the [character/syllable unit + tone number] sequence.

Pinyin	Characters	Functions	English meaning	Lesson
bǐ	筆	n	pen, pencil, brush-pen	5**, 13
bǐ jiào	比較	adv, v-act	comparatively, to compare	25**
biǎo	錶	n	watch	17**
bié	別	adv	don't	19
bīngxié	冰鞋	n	skating boots, skates	28
bìng	病	n, v-state	illness, disease, to fall ill	27**
búcuò	不錯	adj	correct, not bad, pretty good	25
bù	不	adv	not, no	3
bù gǎndāng	不敢當	idiom	I don't really deserve it.	15
Bùlǎng	布朗	n-prop	Brown	21*
cáipàn	裁判	n, v-act	referee, to act as a referee	28
cài	菜	n	dish, vegetable	25**, 27
cān guān	參觀	v-act	to visit, to pay a visit	23
cān jiā	參加	v-act	to take part in, to attend	20
cān tīng	餐廳	n	dining-hall	22
cān zàn	參贊	n	counsellor	27
cè suǒ	廁所	n	toilet, lavatory	10**
céng	層	measure	story (of a building)	10
chá	茶	n	tea	8
chà	差	v-state	to be short of, to lack	17
cháng	嘗	v-act	to taste	27
cháng	常	adv	often	12
Cháng jiāng	長	n-prop	The Yangtze River	7*
chàng	唱	v-act	to sing	19
chàngpiàn	唱片	n	gramophone record	19**
Cháoxiǎn	朝鮮	n-prop	Korea	9**
chē	車	n	car	5
chènshān	襯衫	n	shirt, blouse	16
chéng	城	n	city, town	23
chéngyǔ	成語	n	proverb, idiom	26

Pinyin	Characters	Functions	English meaning	Lesson
chī	吃	v-act	to eat	18
chǐ	尺	n	ruler	5**
chū fā	出發	v-act	to start out, to set off	23
chú fáng	厨房	n	kitchen	22
chuān	穿	v-act	to put on, to wear	16
chuán	船	n	ship	29**
chuāng hu	窗户	n	window	22**
chuáng	床	n	bed	18
cí	詞	n	word	24
cí diǎn	詞典	n	dictionary	11
cóng	從	co-v	from	16
kā fēi guǎn	咖啡館	n	café	17
dǎ cuò le	打錯了	idiom	to have dialled the wrong #	23**
dǎ diànhuà	打電話	v-act	to make a telephone call	23
dà	大	adj, v-state	big, large, to be big	16
dà jiā	大家	pron	all, everybody	27
dà shǐ	大使	n	ambassador	27
dà shǐ guǎn	大使館	n	embassy	27
Dà yáng Zhōu	大洋洲	n-prop	Oceanaria	7**
dà yī	大衣	n	overcoat, topcoat	16**
dài biǎo	代表	n	delegate, representative	23
dài biǎotuán	代表團	n	delegation	23
dài fu	大夫	n	doctor	5
dāng	當	v-id	to act as, to serve as	26
dào	到	v-act	to go, to arrive, to reach	27
de	的	particle	(a structural particle)	5
de	得	particle	(a structural particle)	25
Dé guó	德國	n-prop	Germany	6**
děng	等	v-act	to wait	17
dì di	弟弟	n	younger brother	3

Pinyin	Characters	Functions	English meaning	Lesson
dì tú	地圖	n	map, atlas	7
dì zhǐ	地址	n	address	20
diǎn	點	measure	o'clock, point	17
diǎn xin	點心	n	light refreshments, pastry	24
diàn huà	電話	n	telephone, telephone call	11**, 23
diàn shì	電視	n	television	23
diàn yǐng	電影	n	film, movie	17
diàn yǐng yuàn	電影院	n	cinema	17**
diào	釣	v-act	to fish with a hook and bait	25
Dīng Yún	丁雲	n-prop	Ding Yun	9*, 13*
dǐng	頂	measure	(measure word for hat)	28
dōng tiān	冬天	n	winter	28
dōng xi	東西	n	thing	30
dǒng	懂	v-cog	to understand	24
dōu	都	adv	all	3
duàn liàn	鍛煉	v-act	to do physical training	24
duì	隊	n	team	28
duì	對	v-state	to be right, to be correct	13
duì bu qǐ	對不起	idiom	I'm sorry	20**
duì miàn	對面	n	opposite	22
duō	多	adj, v-st, adv	many, much, a lot of, how	18, 21
duō shao	多少	pron	how many, how much	10
ér zi	兒子	n	son	21**
èr	二	number	two	10
Fǎ guó	法國	n-prop	France	6**, 13**
Fǎ yǔ	法語	n	French	12
fān yì	翻譯	n, v-act	interpreter, to interpret	26
fàn	飯	n	meal, cooked rice, food	18
fáng jiān	房間	n	room	22
fáng zi	房子	n	house	22

Pinyin	Characters	Functions	English meaning	Lesson
fǎng wèn	訪問	v-act	to visit, to call on	23
fàng xīn	放心	idiom	to set one's mind at rest	29
fēi cháng	非常	adv	extremely	21
fēi jī	飛機	n	aeroplane, plane, aircraft	29
Fēi Zhōu	非洲	n-prop	Africa	7**
fēn	分	measure	minute	17
fēn bié	分別	v-act	to part	29
fēn jī	分機	n	extension	23**
fū ren	夫人	n	lady, madame, Mrs.	27
fú wùyuán	服務員	n	waiter, waitress, attendant	19
fǔ dǎo	輔導	v-act	to coach	20
fù xí	復習	v-act	to review	23
gān bēi	乾杯	idiom	to propose a toast, here's to...	27
gān jìng	乾淨	adj, v-state	clean, neat, to be clean	21**
gǎn xiè	感謝	v-act	to thank	21
gāo xìng	高興	adj, v-state	happy, to be delighted	21
gào su	告訴	v-act	to tell	14
gē-r	歌兒	n	song	19
gē ge	哥哥	n	elder brother	3
gē jù	歌劇	n	opera	26**
ge	個	measure	a measure word	15
gěi	給	co-v, v-act	for, to, to give	14
gēn	跟	co-v, v-act	with, to follow	17
gèng	更	adv	even, still	21
gōng chǎng	工廠	n	factory	23
gōng chéng shī	工程師	n	engineer	14**
gōng ping	公平	adj	fair	28
gōng rén	工人	n	worker	23
gōng sī	公司	n	company	14**
gōng yuán	公園	n	park	28**

Pinyin	Characters	Functions	English meaning	Lesson
gōng zuò	工作	n, v	work, to work	14
gū niang	姑娘	n	girl	21
Gǔ bō	古波	n-prop	Gubo	1*, 13*
gǔ diǎn	古典	n	classical, classic	19
guì xìng	貴姓	idiom	What's your name?	9
Guō Mòruò	郭沫若	n-prop	Guo Moruo	26*
guó	國	n	country, state	6
guó jiā	國家	n	country	30
guò	過	v-act	to live, to get along	30
hái	還	adv	still, in addition, else	15
hái shì	還是	conj	or	19
hái zi	孩子	n	child	14
Hàn yǔ	漢語	n	Chinese (language)	6
Hàn zì	漢字	n	Chinese character	15
hǎo	好	adj, v-state	good, to be good, to be well	1
hǎo kàn	好看	adj, v-state	good-looking, to be beautiful	21
hào	號	n	number, date, day of the month	10, 20
hào mǎ	號碼	n	number	23**
hē	喝	v-act	to drink	8
hé	河	n	river	25
hé	和	conj	and, with	13
hēi	黑	adj, v-state	black, to be black	16**
hěn	很	adv	very	2
hóng	紅	adj, v-state	red, to be red	19
hóng chá	紅茶	n	black tea	19
hòu biān	後邊	n	back, at the back of, behind	22
hù xiāng	互相	adv	each other, mutually	15
huā chá	花茶	n	scented tea, jasmine tea	19
huā-r	花兒	n	flower	21
huā yuán	花園	n	garden	22

Pinyin	Characters	Functions	English meaning	Lesson
huá bīng	滑冰	v-comb	to skate, skating	28
huá xuě	滑雪	v-comb	to ski, skiing	28**
huà	畫	v-act	to paint, to draw	26**
huà bào	畫報	n	pictorial	11
huà-r	畫兒	n	painting, drawing, picture	26**
huān yíng	歡迎	v-act	to welcome	8
huán	還	v-act	to return	11
Huáng Hé	黃河	n-prop	The Yellow River	7*
huí	回	v-act	to return	17
huí dá	回答	v-act	to reply, to answer	24
huì	會	aux v	to know how to, can	26
huǒ chē	火車	n	train	24
huǒ tuǐ	火腿	n	ham	25
huò zhě	或者	conj	or	26
jī chǎng	機場	n	airfield, airport	29
jī dàn	鷄蛋	n	hen's egg	25**
jǐ	幾	number, pron	several, how many, how much	15
jiā	家	n	family, home, house	14
jiā shēn	加深	v-act	to deepen	26
jiàn	見	v-act	to meet, to see	29
jiàn	件	measure	a measure word	16
jiàn kāng	健	adj, n, v-state	healthy, health, to be healthy	27
jiàn miàn	見面	v-comb	to meet (to see) each other	29
jiāo	教	v-act	to teach	15
jiǎo zi	餃子	n	Chinese dumpling	25**
jiào	叫	v-id, v-act	to be called, to hire, to call	9, 29**
jiào liàn	教練	n	coach, trainer	25
jiào shì	教室	n	classroom	15**
jiào shòu	教授	n	professor	13**
jiē diàn huà	接電話	v-act	to answer a phone	23

180

Pinyin	Characters	Functions	English meaning	Lesson
jiē (rén)	接(人)	v-act	to meet one at a station/airport	23
jié hūn	結婚	v-comb	to get married	20**
jiě jie	姐姐	n	elder sister	14
jiè	借	v-act	to borrow, to lend	15**
jiè shào	介紹	v-act	to introduce	13
jīn nián	今年	n	this year	20
jīn tiān	今天	n	today	20
jǐn	緊	adj	close, tight, taut	29
jìn	進	v-act	to enter, to come in	8
jìn bù	進步	n, v-act	progress, to make progress	29
jìn lái	進來	v-comb	to come in, to enter	26**
jīng jù	京劇	n	Beijing opera	16
jīng lǐ	經理	n	manager, director	14**
jiǔ	酒	n	wine	27
jiǔ	九	number	nine	11
jiù	就	adv, conj	at once, right away	26
jiù	舊	adj, v-state	old, to be old	16
jú zi	橘子	n	orange	19
jú zi shuǐ	橘子水	n	orangeade, orange juice	19
jù chǎng	劇場	n	theatre	16**
kā fēi	咖啡	n	coffee	8**, 17
kāi	開	v-act	to open	21
kāi (chē)	開(車)	v-act	to drive (a car)	23
kāi shǐ	開始	v-act	to begin, to start	27
kàn	看	v-act	to look, to read, to watch	7
kě shì	可是	conj	but	26
kě yǐ	可以	aux v	may	26
kè	刻	measure	quarter (or an hour)	17
kè	課	n	class	17
kè qi	客氣	adj, v-state	polite, to be polite	8

181

Pinyin	Characters	Functions	English meaning	Lesson
kè tīng	客廳	n	drawing room, parlour	22
kè wén	課文	n	text	23
kòng-r	空兒	n	spare time	20
kǒu yǔ	口語	n	spoken language	15
kū	哭	v-act	to cry, to weep	30
kù zi	褲子	n	trousers	16**
kuài	快	adj	fast, quick	25
kuài zi	筷子	n	chopsticks	27
kuàng quán shuǐ	礦泉水	n	mineral water	25
lái	來	v-act	to come	13
lán	藍	adj, v-state	blue, to be blue	16**
lán qiú	籃球	n	basketball	28**
lǎo	老	adj., v-state	old, to be old	6
lǎo shī	老師	n	teacher	6
le	了	particle	(a modal particle)	13
lí	離	prep	from	30
lí kāi	離開	v-act	to leave	29
Lǐ	李	n-prop	Li	27*
lǐ biān	裏邊	n	inside	22
lǐ wù	禮物	n	present, gift	21**
lǐ xiǎng	理想	n, adj	ideal	26
liǎ	倆	m	both, two	26
liàn xí	練習	n, v-act	exercise, to practice	24
liǎng	兩	number	two	16
liàng	輛	measure	measure word for vehicle	21**
liǎo jiě	了解	v-cog	to understand, to know	26
líng	零	number	zero	10
liú lì	流利	adj	fluent	25**
liú xué shēng	留學生	n	a foreign student	9
liù	六	number	six	11

182

Pinyin	Characters	Functions	English meaning	Lesson
lóu	樓	n	storied building, floor	27
Lǔ Xùn	魯迅	n-prop	Lu Xun	26*
lù	路	n	road, way	17
lǜ	綠	adj, v-state	green, to be green	16
lǜ chá	綠茶	n	green tea	19**
ma	嗎	particle	(an interrogative particle)	2
māma	媽媽	n	mother	4
Mǎ lǐ	馬里	n-prop	Mali	6**
mǎi	買	v-act	to buy	13
màn	慢	adj	slow	25
máng	忙	adj, v-state	busy, to be busy	3
máo táijiǔ	茅台酒	n	Maotai (a Chinese liquor)	27
mào zi	帽子	n	hat, cap	28
méi	沒	adv, v-poss	not, no, do not have	14
méi guān xi	沒關係	idiom	it doesn't matter	20**
méi (you)	沒(有)	adv	not, no	23
měi	每	pron	every, each	18
Měi guó	美國	n-prop	U.S.A.	6**
mèi mei	妹妹	n	younger sister	14
mén	門	n	door	21
miàn bāo	麵包	n	bread	25
mín gē	民歌	n	folk song	19
míng nián	明年	n	next year	20**, 29
míng tiān	明天	n	tomorrow	23
míng zi	名字	n	name	13
nǎ	哪	pron	which	6
nǎr	哪兒	pron	where	10
nǎ li	哪裏	idiom	it is nothing	25
nà	那	pron	that	5
nà-r	那兒	pron	there	10**, 15

183

Pinyin	Characters	Functions	English meaning	Lesson
nǎi lào	奶酪	n	cheese	25
nán	難	adj, v-state	difficult, to be difficult	24
nán	男	adj	male	13
nán guò	難過	adj	sad	29
Nán Měi Zhōu	南美洲	n-prop	South America	7**
ne	呢	particle	(a modal particle)	2
néng	能	aux v	can, to be able to	26
nǐ	你	pron	you	1
nǐ men	你們	pron	you (pl.)	4
nián	年	n	year	20
nián qīng	年輕	adj, v-state	young, to be young	21
niàn	念	v-act	to read (aloud), to study	24
nín	您	pron	you (polite form of "nǐ")	8
niú nǎi	牛奶	n	(cows) milk	8**, 25**
nóng cūn	農村	n	countryside, rural areas	24
nóng mín	農民	n	peasant	24
nǔ lì	努力	adj	hard-working, studious	29
nǚ	女	adj	female	12
nǚ ér	女兒	n	daughter	21**, 30
nǚ shì	女士	n	polite address to a lady	9**
Ōu Zhōu	歐洲	n-prop	Europe	7**
Pà lán kǎ	帕蘭卡	n-prop	Palanka	1*, 13**
pái qiú	排球	n	volleyball	28**
páng biān	旁邊	n	side	22
péng you	朋友	n	friend	4
pí jiǔ	啤酒	n	beer	8**, 19
piào	票	n	ticket	16
piào liang	漂亮	adj, v-state	pretty, beautiful, to be pretty	21
pīng pāng qiú	乒乓球	n	table tennis	28**
píng	瓶	measure	bottle	19

Pinyin	Characters	Functions	English meaning	Lesson
píng guǒ	蘋果	n	apple	19**
pú tao	葡萄	n	grape	19**, 27
pú tao jiǔ	葡萄酒	n	grape wine	27
qī	七	number	seven	11
qǐ	起	v-act	to get up, to rise	18
qǐ chuáng	起床	idiom	to get up	18
qǐ fēi	起飛	v-act	to take off	29
qì chē	汽車	n	car, vehicle	29**
qì rén	氣人	idiom	to get someone angry/annoyed	28
qiān zhèng	簽證	n	visa	28
qián biān	前邊	n	front, in front of, before	22**, 25
qīng chu	清楚	adj	clear, distinct	25**
qǐng	請	v-act	please	8
qǐng wèn	請問	idiom	May I ask...?	9
qiū tiān	秋天	n	autumn	29
qiú	球	n	ball	28
qù	去	v-act	to go	12
qù nián	去年	n	last year	20**, 30
qún zi	裙子	n	skirt	16
ràng	讓	v-act	to let, to ask	19
rè qíng	熱情	adj	cordial, enthusiastic	30
rén	人	n	person	6
rén mín	人民	n	people	26
Rén mín Rì bào	人民日報	n-prop	The People's Daily	23*
rèn shi	認識	v-cog	to know, to recognize	12
rèn zhēn	認真	adj, v-state	conscientious, (to be) serious	24
rì	日	n	date, day of the month	20
Rì běn	日本	n-prop	Japan	6**, 21*
róng yi	容易	adj	easy	26
sài	賽	n, v-act	competition, match, to compete	28

Pinyin	Characters	Functions	English meaning	Lesson
sān	三	number	three	10
shāng diàn	商店	n	shop	13
shàng	上	v-act	to get on, to get into, to board	29
shàng bān	上班	idiom	to go to work	17**
shàng biān	上邊	n	top, on, over, above	22
Shàng hǎi	上海	n-prop	Shanghai	7*
shàng (kè)	上課	v-act	to attend or to teach (a class)	17
shàng wǔ	上午	n	morning	18
shàng yī	上衣	n	upper outer garment	16**
shǎo	少	adj, v-state	few, little, to be few	22
Cháng chéng	長城	n-prop	The Great Wall	7*
shéi	誰	pron	who	6
shēn tǐ	身體	n	body, health	29
shén me	甚麼	pron	what	7
shēng cí	生詞	n	new word	15**, 24
shēng ri	生日	n	birthday	20
shī gē	詩歌	n	poem	26**
shí	十	number	ten	11
shí táng	食堂	n	dining-hall	17
shí yànshì	實驗室	n	laboratory	15**
shì	試	v-act	to try	27
shì	是	v-id	to be	4
shì-r	事兒	n	business, thing	17
shì jiè	世界	n	world	7**
shū	書	n	book	5
shū	輸	v-act	to lose	28
shū diàn	書店	n	bookstore	14
shū fáng	書房	n	study	22
shù	束	measure	bunch	21
shuāng	雙	measure	pair	28

Pinyin	Characters	Functions	English meaning	Lesson
shuǐ	水	n	water	19
shuì jiào	睡覺	idiom	to go to bed, to sleep	18
shuō	説	v-act	to speak, to say	13
sì	四	number	four	10
sòng	送	v-act	to give, to give as a present	21
sòng (rén)	送 (人)	v(-comb)-act	to see (someone) off	30
sòng xíng	送行	v-act	to see someone off	29**
sù shè	宿舍	n	dormitory	10
suì	歲	measure	year (age)	20
suì shu	歲數	n	age	21**
suǒ yǐ	所以	conj	so, therefore, as a result	29
tā	他	pron	he, him	3
tā	她	pron	she, her	5
tāmen	他們	pron	they, them	3
tāmen	她們	pron	they, them (for females)	12
tài	太	adv	too, too much	16
tài tai	太太	n	Mrs., madame	8**, 21
tán	談	v-act	to talk, to chat	20**, 26
tāng	湯	n	soup	25
táng	糖	n	sugar, sweets, candy	19**
tào	套	measure	set	22**
tī	踢	v-act	to kick	28
tǐ yù chǎng	體育場	n	stadium	28**
tiān	天	n	day	18
tiáo	條	measure	a measure word	16
tiào wǔ	跳舞	v-comb	to dance	21
tīng	聽	v-act	to listen	19
tíng	停	v-act	to stop, to come to a stop	25
tóng xué	同學	n	classmate, schoolmate	20
tóng zhì	同志	n	comrade	9**

Pinyin	Characters	Functions	English meaning	Lesson
tú shū guǎn	圖書館	n	library	15
yùn dòng	運動	v-act	to exercise, to work out	28**
wài biān	外邊	n	outside	22**, 23
wài yǔ	外語	n	foreign language	9
wán-r	玩兒	v-act	to play, to have fun with	23
wǎn	晚	adj	late	25
wǎn fàn	晚飯	n	supper, dinner	26**
wǎn shang	晚上	n	evening	16
Wáng	王	n-prop	Wang	8*, 15*
Wáng Shūwén	王書文	n-prop	Wang Shuwen	24*
wǎng qiú	網球	n	tennis	28**
wàng	忘	v-act	to forget	29
wèi	位	measure	measure word	25
wèi	爲	prep	for, to	27
wèi	喂	interj	hello	13
wén huà	文化	n	culture	27
wén xué	文學	n	literature	26
wèn	問	v-act	to ask	9
wèn tí	問題	n	question	18
wǒ	我	pron	I, me	2
wǒ men	我們	pron	we, us	6
wò shì	臥室	n	bedroom	22
wǔ	五	number	five	10
wǔ fàn	午飯	n	lunch	28
wǔ guān	武官	n	military attaché	27**
wǔ huì	舞會	n	dance, ball	20
xī yān	吸煙(烟)	v-act	to smoke	8
xǐ huan	喜歡	v-act	to like, to be fond of	19
xǐ zǎo	洗澡	v-act	to take a bath	22
xǐ zǎo jiān	洗澡間	n	bathroom	22

Pinyin	Characters	Functions	English meaning	Lesson
xì	系	n	department, faculty	15
xià bān	下班	idiom	to come or go off work	17**
xià biān	下邊	n	bottom	22**
xià (kè)	下課	v-act	class is over or dismissed	17
xià tiān	夏天	n	summer	29
xià wǔ	下午	n	afternoon	18
xiān sheng	先生	n	Mr., sir, gentleman	8**, 12
xiàn dài	現代	n	modern	19
xiàn zài	現在	n	now, nowadays	11
xiāng bīn jiǔ	香檳酒	n	champagne	27**
xiāng jiāo	香蕉	n	banana	19**
xiāng zi	箱子	n	suitcase	28
xiǎng	想	v-act, v-int	to miss, to think, to want	14
xiàng	像	v-id	to be like, to resemble	21
xiǎo	小	adj, v-state	little, small, to be small	22
xiǎo jie	小姐	n	miss, young lady	9**, 19
xiǎo shuō	小說	n	novel	26**
xiǎo xué shēng	小學生	n	pupil, schoolboy/girl	27**
xiào	笑	v-act	to laugh, to smile	30
xiē	些	measure	some	24
xié	鞋	n	shoes	28
xiě	寫	v-act	to write	14
xiè xie	謝謝	v-act	to thank	8
xīn	心	n	heart	30
xīn	新	adj, v-state	new, to be new	15
xīn nián	新年	n	New Year	21**
xīn wén	新聞	n	news	23
xìn	信	n	letter	14
xīng qī	星期	n	week	20
xīng qī rì	星期日	n	Sunday	20

Pinyin	Characters	Functions	English meaning	Lesson
xíng li	行李	n	luggage, baggage	28
xìng	姓	n, v-id	a surname, (one's) surname is	9
xiū xi	休息	v-act	to take a rest	18
xué	學	v-act	to study, to learn	9
xué sheng	學生	n	student	9
xué xí	學習	v-act	to study, to learn	9
xué yuàn	學院	n	college, institute	9
lǚ xíng	旅行	v-act	to travel, to tour	29**
yān	煙(烟)	n	cigarette, smoke	8
yán jiu	研究	n, v-act	research, to research, to study	26
yào	要	v-act, v-int	to want; must, to be going to	19
yào	要	aux v	will, to be going to	29
yě	也	adv	also, too	2
yī	一	number	one	10
yī mì	一秘	n	first secretary	27**
yī yuàn	醫院	n	hospital	10**
yí dìng	一定	adj, adv	particular, surely, certainly	20
yí lù píng ān	一路平安	idiom	to have a pleasant journey	29
yí xiàr	一下兒	idiom	a little while	11
yǐ hòu	以後	n	later on, in the future	17
yǐ qián	以前	n	before, in the past, ago	17**
yǐ zi	椅子	n	chair	22
yì diǎnr	一點兒	idiom	a little, a bit	25
yì qǐ	一起	adv	together	17
yīn yuè	音樂	n	music	19
yīn yuè huì	音樂會	n	concert	20**
yín háng	銀行	n	bank	14
yīng gāi	應該	aux v	should, ought to	26
Yīng guó	英國	n-prop	Britain	9**, 13**
Yīng yǔ	英語	n	English	12

Pinyin	Characters	Functions	English meaning	Lesson
yíng	贏	v-act	to beat, to win	28
yòng	用	v-act	to use, to make use of	11
yóu jú	郵局	n	post office	13**
yóu piào	郵票	n	stamp	13**
yóu yǒng	游泳	v-comb	to swim, swimming	25
yǒu	有	v-poss	to have, there be	14
yǒu hǎo	友好	adj, v-state	friendly, to be friendly	23
yǒu míng	有名	adj	famous, well-known	26
yǒu shí hou	有時候	idiom	sometimes	18
yǒu yì	友誼	n	friendship	27
yǒu yì si	有意思	idiom	interesting	20
yòu	又	adv	again, in addition to, more	27
yòu biān	右邊	n	right	22**
yú	魚	n	fish	25
yǔ fǎ	語法	n	grammar	15
yǔ sǎn	雨傘	n	umbrella	11**
yuǎn	遠	adj	far, distant	30
yuàn yì	願意	v-int	to be willing	29
yuē huì	約會	n	appointment	20**
yuè	月	n	month	20
yuè lǎn shì	閱覽室	n	reading room	15
yùn dòng	運動	n	sports	28**
zá zhì	雜誌	n	magazine	11**, 15
zài	再	adv	again, once more	25
zài	在	v-loc	to be at, to be in	10
zài jiàn	再見	idiom	See you again; Good bye	11
zǎo	早	adj	early	26
zǎo fàn	早飯	n	breakfast	28
zěn me yàng	怎麼樣	idiom	how is it	22
zhàn	站	v-act	to stand	29
zhàn xiàn	佔綫	idiom	the line is busy	23**

Pinyin	Characters	Functions	English meaning	Lesson
zhāng	張	measure	piece	16
zhāo dài huì	招待會	n	reception	27
zhǎo	找	v-act	to look for, to call on (a person)	16
zhào piàn	照片	n	photograph, picture	21**, 23
zhào xiàng	照像(相)	v-comb	to take a picture	29
zhè	這	pron	this	4
zhè-r	這兒	pron	here	10**, 16
zhēn	真	adj	real, true, genuine	21
zhěng lǐ	整理	v-act	to put in order, to straighten up	22
zhěng qí	整齊	adj, v-state	tidy, to be tidy	25**
zhèng zài	正在	adv	(action in progress)	23
zhī	枝	measure	branch, etc.	19**
zhī dao	知道	v-cog	to know	20
zhí yuán	職員	n	office worker, staff	14**
zhǐ	紙	n	paper	5**, 13
zhōng	鐘	n	clock	17**
Zhōng guó	中國	n-prop	China	6*, 13*
Zhōng guó Mínháng	中國民航	n-prop	CAAC	29**
zhōng jiān	中間	n	middle	22**
Zhōng wén	中文	n	Chinese (language)	15
zhù	祝	v-act	to wish	21
zhù	住	v-loc	to live	10
zhù hè	祝賀	n, v-act	congratulation, to congratulate	20
zhù yì	注意	v-act	to pay attention to	29
zhǔn bèi	準備	v-act	to prepare	25
zhuō zi	桌子	n	table	22
zì	字	n	character	15
zì jǐ	自己	pron	self	30
zǒng	總	adv	always	22
zǒng jī	總機	n	central exchange, switchboard	23**

Pinyin	Characters	Functions	English meaning	Lesson
zǒng shì	總是	adv	always	22
zǒu	走	v-act	to go, to walk	17
zú qiú	足球	n	football	28
zuó tiān	昨天	n	yesterday	28
zuǒ biān	左邊	n	left	22
zuò	坐	v-act	to sit, to take a seat	10
zuò	作	v-act	to do	14
zuòjiā	作家	n	writer	26
zuòwèi	座位	n	seat	16**

PCR I Vocabulary

English Sequence

English meaning	Pinyin	Characters	Functions	Lesson
a little	yì diǎnr	一點兒	idiom	25
a little while	yíxiàr	一下兒	idiom	11
above	shàngbiān	上邊	n	22
across from	duì miàn	對面	n	22
address	dì zhǐ	地址	n	20
advance	jìnbù	進步	n	29
aeroplane	fēijī	飛機	n	29
Africa	Fēi Zhōu	非洲	n-prop	7**
afternoon	xiàwǔ	下午	n	18
again	yòu	又	adv	27
again	zài	再	adv	25
age	suì shu	歲數	n	21**
ago	yǐqián	以前	n	17**
aircraft, airplane	fēijī	飛機	n	29
airport	jīchǎng	機場	n	29
all	dōu	都	adv	3
all	dàjiā	大家	pron	27
also	yě	也	adv	2
always	zǒng(shì)	總(是)	adv	22
ambassador	dàshǐ	大使	n	27
America	Měiguó	美國	n-prop	6**
and	hé	和	conj	13
Anna	Ānnà	安娜	n-prop	24*

English meaning	Pinyin	Characters	Functions	Lesson
apple	píngguǒ	蘋果	n	19**
appointment	yuēhuì	約會	n	20**
as a result	suǒyǐ	所以	conj	29
at once	jiù	就	adv	26
atlas	dìtú	地圖	n	7
attendant	fúwùyuán	服務員	n	19
autumn	qiūtiān	秋天	n	29
back	hòubiān	後邊	n	22
baggage	xíngli	行李	n	28
ball	qiú	球	n	28
ball	wǔhuì	舞會	n	20
banana	xiāngjiāo	香蕉	n	19**
bank	yínháng	銀行	n	14
basketball	lánqiú	籃球	n	28**
bathroom	xǐzǎojiān	洗澡間	n	22
beautiful	piàoliang	漂亮	adj	21
bed	chuáng	床	n	18
bedroom	wòshì	臥室	n	22
beer	píjiǔ	啤酒	n	8**, 19
before	yǐqián	以前	n	17**
Beijing	Běijīng	北京	n-prop	7*, 18*
Beijing opera	jīngjù	京劇	n	16
big	dà	大	adj	16
birthday	shēngri	生日	n	20
black	hēi	黑	adj	16**
black tea	hóngchá	紅茶	n	19
blouse	chènshān	襯衫	n	16
blue	lán	藍	adj	16**
body	shēntǐ	身體	n	29
book	shū	書	n	5
bookstore	shūdiàn	書店	n	14

English meaning	Pinyin	Characters	Functions	Lesson
both	liǎ	倆	measure	26
bottle	píng	瓶	measure	19
bottom	xiàbian	下邊	n	22**
branch, etc.	zhī	枝	measure	19**
brandy	báilándì	白蘭地	n	27**
bread	miànbāo	麵包	n	25
breakfast	zǎofàn	早飯	n	28
Britain	Yīngguó	英國	n-prop	9**, 13**
Brown	Bùlǎng	布朗	n-prop	21*
brush-pen	bǐ	筆	n	5**, 13
bunch	shù	束	measure	21
business	shìr	事兒	n	17
busy	máng	忙	adj	3
but	kěshì	可是	conj	26
CAAC	Zhōngguó Mínháng	中國民航	n-prop	29**
café	kāfēiguǎn	咖啡館	n	17
can	huì	會	aux v	26
candy	táng	糖	n	19**
cap	màozi	帽子	n	28
car	chē	車	n	5
car	qìchē	汽車	n	29**
central exchange	zǒngjī	總機	n	23**
certainly	yídìng	一定	adv	20
chair	yǐzi	椅子	n	22
champagne	xiāngbīnjiǔ	香檳酒	n	27**
character	zì	字	n	15
cheese	nǎilào	奶酪	n	25
child	háizi	孩子	n	14
China	Zhōngguó	中國	n-prop	6*, 13*
Chinese (language)	Zhōngwén	中文	n	15
Chinese (oral language)	Hànyǔ	漢語	n	6

English meaning	Pinyin	Characters	Functions	Lesson
Chinese character	Hànzì	漢字	n	15
Chinese dumpling	jiǎozi	餃子	n	25**
chopsticks	kuàizi	筷子	n	27
cigarette	yān	煙(烟)	n	8
cinema	diànyǐngyuàn	電影院	n	17**
city, town	chéng	城	n	23
class	kè	課	n	17
class	bān	班	n	15**, 20
class is over or dismissed	xià(kè)	下課	v-comb	17
classic, classical	gǔdiǎn	古典	n	19
classmate	tóngxué	同學	n	20
classroom	jiàoshì	教室	n	15**
clean	gānjìng	乾淨	adj	21**
clear	qīngchu	清楚	adj	25**
clock	zhōng	鐘	n	17**
close	jǐn	緊	adj	29
coach	jiàoliàn	教練	n	25
coffee	kāfēi	咖啡	n	8**, 17
college	xuéyuàn	學院	n	9
company	gōngsī	公司	n	14**
comparatively	bǐjiào	比較	adv	25**
comparing to...	bǐ	比	prep	28
competition	sài	賽	n	28
comrade	tóngzhì	同志	n	9**
concert	yīnyuèhuì	音樂會	n	20**
congratulation	zhùhè	祝賀	n	20
conscientious	rènzhēn	認真	adj	24
contemporary	xiàndài	現代	n	19
cooked rice	fàn	飯	n	18
cordial	rèqíng	熱情	adj	30
correct	búcuò	不錯	adj	25

English meaning	Pinyin	Characters	Functions	Lesson
counselor	cānzàn	參贊	n	27
country	guójiā	國家	n	30
country	guó	國	n	6
countryside	nóngcūn	農村	n	24
culture	wénhuà	文化	n	27
cup	bēi	杯	measure	19
dance	wǔhuì	舞會	n	20
dancing party	wǔhuì	舞會	n	20
date	hào, rì	號, 日	n	20
daughter	nǚ'ér	女兒	n	21**, 30
day	tiān	天	n	18
day of the month	hào, rì	號, 日	n	20
delegate	dàibiǎo	代表	n	23
delegation	dàibiǎotuán	代表團	n	23
department	xì	系	n	15
dialed the wrong number	dǎ cuò le	打錯了	idiom	23**
dictionary	cídiǎn	詞典	n	11
difficult	nán	難	adj	24
Ding Yun	Dīng Yún	丁雲	n-prop	9*, 13*
dining-hall	cāntīng	餐廳	n	22
dining-hall	shítáng	食堂	n	17
dinner	wǎnfàn	晚飯	n	26**
director	jīnglǐ	經理	n	14**
disease	bìng	病	n	27**
dish	cài	菜	n	25**, 27
distant	yuǎn	遠	adj	30
distinct	qīngchu	清楚	adj	25**
do not have	méi	沒	v-poss	14
doctor	dàifu	大夫	n	5
don't	bié	別	adv	19

English meaning	Pinyin	Characters	Functions	Lesson
door	mén	門	n	21
dormitory	sùshè	宿舍	n	10
drawing	huàr	畫兒	n	26**
drawing room	kètīng	客聽	n	22
each	měi	每	pron	18
each other	hùxiāng	互相	adv	15
early	zǎo	早	adj	26
easy	róngyì	容易	adj	26
eight	bā	八	number	11
elder brother	gēge	哥哥	n	3
elder sister	jiějie	姐姐	n	14
else	hái	還	adv	15
embassy	dàshǐguǎn	大使館	n	27
engineer	gōngchéngshī	工程師	n	14**
English language	Yīngyǔ	英語	n	12
enthusiastic	rèqíng	熱情	adj	30
Europe	Ōu Zhōu	歐洲	n-prop	7**
even, still	gèng	更	adv	21
evening	wǎnshang	晚上	n	16
every	měi	每	pron	18
everybody	dàjiā	大家	pron	27
exchange student	liúxuéshēng	留學生	n	9
excited	gāoxìng	高興	adj	21
exercise	liànxí	練習	n	24
extension	fēnjī	分機	n	23**
extraordinarily	fēicháng	非常	adv	21
extremely	fēicháng	非常	adv	21
factory	gōngchǎng	工廠	n	23
faculty	xì	系	n	15
fair	gōngping	公平	adj	28
family	jiā	家	n	14

English meaning	Pinyin	Characters	Functions	Lesson
famous	yǒumíng	有名	adj	26
far	yuǎn	遠	adj	30
fast	kuài	快	adj	25
father	bàba	爸爸	n	4
female	nǚ	女	adj	12
few	shǎo	少	adj	22
film	diànyǐng	電影	n	17
first secretary	yīmì	一秘	n	27**
fish	yú	魚	n	25
five	wǔ	五	number	10
floor	lóu	樓	n	27
flower	huār	花兒	n	21
fluent	liúlì	流利	adj	25**
folk song	míngē	民歌	n	19
food	fàn	飯	n	18
football	zúqiú	足球	n	28
for	wèi	爲	prep	27
for	gěi	給	co-v	14
foreign language	wàiyǔ	外語	n	9
foreign student	liúxuéshēng	留學生	n	9
four	sì	四	number	10
France	Fǎguó	法國	n-prop	6**, 13**
French	Fǎyǔ	法語	n	12
friend	péngyou	朋友	n	4
friendly	yǒuhǎo	友好	adj	23
friendship	yǒuyì	友誼	n	27
from	cóng	從	co-v	16
from	lí	離	prep	30
front	qiánbiān	前邊	n	22**, 25
garden	huāyuán	花園	n	22
gentleman	xiānsheng	先生	n	8**, 12

English meaning	Pinyin	Characters	Functions	Lesson
genuine	zhēn	真	adj	21
Germany	Déguó	德國	n-prop	6**
gift	lǐwù	禮物	n	21**
girl	gūniang	姑娘	n	21
Good bye	zàijiàn	再見	idiom	11
Good morning!	zǎo	早	adj	26
good	hǎo	好	adj	1
good-looking	hǎokàn	好看	adj	21
grammar	yǔfǎ	語法	n	15
gramophone record	chàngpiàn	唱片	n	19**
grape	pútao	葡萄	n	19**, 27
grape wine	pútaojiǔ	葡萄酒	n	27
green	lǜ	綠	adj, v-state	16
green tea	lǜchá	綠茶	n	19**
Gubo	Gǔbō	古波	n-prop	1*, 13*
Guo Moruo	Guō Mòruò	郭沫若	n-prop	26*
half	bàn	半	number	17
ham	huǒtuǐ	火腿	n	25
happy	gāoxìng	高興	adj	21
hard-working	nǔlì	努力	adj	29
hat	màozi	帽子	n	28
he	tā	他	pron	3
health	shēntǐ	身體	n	29
health	jiànkāng	健康	n	27
healthy	jiànkāng	健康	adj	27
heart	xīn	心	n	30
hello	wèi	喂	interj	13
help	bāngzhu	幫助	n	22
hen's egg	jīdàn	鷄蛋	n	25**
her	tā	她	pron	5

English meaning	Pinyin	Characters	Functions	Lesson
here	zhèr	這兒	pron	10**, 16
here's to...	gān bēi	乾杯	idiom	27
him	tā	他	pron	3
home	jiā	家	n	14
hospital	yīyuàn	醫院	n	10**
house	jiā	家	n	√14
house	fángzi	房子	n	22
how	duō	多	adv	21
how is it	zěnmeyàng	怎麼樣	idiom	22
how many (much)	duōshao	多少	pron	10
how many, how much	jǐ	幾	pron	15
husband	xiānsheng	先生	n	8**, 12
I	wǒ	我	pron	2
I don't really deserve it.	bù gǎndāng	不敢當	idiom	15
I'm sorry	duì bu qǐ	對不起	idiom	20**
ideal	lǐxiǎng	理想	adj, n	26
idiom	chéngyǔ	成語	n	26
illness	bìng	病	n	27**
in addition	hái	還	adv	15
in addition to	yòu	又	adv	27
in the midst of	zhèngzài	正在	adv	23
inside	lǐbiān	裏邊	n	22
institute	xuéyuàn	學院	n	9
interesting	yǒu yì si	有意思	idiom	20
interpreter	fānyì	翻譯	n	26
it doesn't matter	méi guānxi	沒關係	idiom	20**
it is nothing	nǎli	哪裏	idiom	25
Japan	Rì běn	日本	n-prop	6**, 21*
jasmine tea	huāchá	花茶	n	19
kitchen	chúfáng	厨房	n	22
Korea	Cháoxiǎn	朝鮮	n-prop	9**

English meaning	Pinyin	Characters	Functions	Lesson
laboratory	shíyànshì	實驗室	n	15**
lady, Madame, Mrs.	fūren	夫人	n	27
last year	qùnián	去年	n	20**, 30
late	wǎn	晚	adj	25
later on, in the future	yǐhòu	以後	n	17
lavatory	cèsuǒ	廁所	n	10**
left	zuǒbiān	左邊	n	22
letter	xìn	信	n	14
Li	Lǐ	李	n-prop	27*
library	túshūguǎn	圖書館	n	15
light refreshments	diǎnxin	點心	n	24
literature	wénxué	文學	n	26
little	shǎo	少	adj	22
little	xiǎo	小	adj	22
living room	kètīng	客廳	n	22
Lu Xun	Lǔ Xùn	魯迅	n-prop	26*
luggage	xíngli	行李	n	28
lunch	wǔfàn	午飯	n	28
Madame	tàitai	太太	n	8**, 21
magazine	zázhì	雜誌	n	11**, 15
male	nán	男	adj	13
Mali	Mǎlǐ	馬里	n-prop	6**
manager	jīnglǐ	經理	n	14**
many	duō	多	adv	21
many	duō	多	adj, v-state	18
Maotai (a strong liquor)	máotáijiǔ	茅台酒	n	27
map	dìtú	地圖	n	7
match	sài	賽	n	28
May I ask...?	qǐngwèn	請問	idiom	9
may	kěyǐ	可以	aux v	26
me	wǒ	我	pron	2

English meaning	Pinyin	Characters	Functions	Lesson
meal	fàn	飯	n	18
middle	zhōngjiān	中間	n	22**
military attaché	wǔguān	武官	n	27**
milk, (cow's)	niúnǎi	牛奶	n	8**, 25**
mineral water	kuàngquánshuǐ	礦泉水	n	25
minute	fēn	分	measure	17
miss	xiǎojie	小姐	n	9**, 19
modern	xiàndài	現代	n	19
month	yuè	月	n	20
more	yòu	又	adv	27
morning	shàngwǔ	上午	n	18
mother	māma	媽媽	n	4
movie	diànyǐng	電影	n	17
Mr.	xiānsheng	先生	n	8**, 12
Mrs.	tàitai	太太	n	8**, 21
much	duō	多	adj, v-state	18
music	yīnyuè	音樂	n	19
must	yào	要	v-int	19
mutually	hùxiāng	互相	adv	15
name	míngzi	名字	n	13
neat	gānjing	乾淨	adj	21**
New Year	xīnnián	新年	n	21**
new	xīn	新	adj	15
new word	shēngcí	生詞	n	15**, 24
news	xīnwén	新聞	n	23
newspaper	bào	報	n	5**, 15
next year	míngnián	明年	n	20**, 29
nine	jiǔ	九	number	11
no, not	bù	不	adv	3
no, not	méi	沒	adv	14

English meaning	Pinyin	Characters	Functions	Lesson
no, not	méi (yǒu)	没 (有)	adv	23
not bad	búcuò	不錯	adj	25
note-book	běnzi	本子	n	11**, 13**
novel	xiǎoshuō	小說	n	26**
now, nowadays	xiànzài	現在	n	11
number	hào	號	n	10
number	hàomǎ	號碼	n	23**
o'clock	diǎn	點	measure	17
Oceanaria	Dàyáng Zhōu	大洋洲	n-prop	7**
office worker	zhíyuán	職員	n	14**
often	cháng	常	adv	12
oh	à	啊	interj	13
old	jiù	舊	adj	16
on	shàngbiān	上邊	n	22
once more	zài	再	adv	25
one	yī	一	number	10
opera	gējù	歌劇	n	26**
opposite	duì miàn	對面	n	22
or	háishi	還是	conj	19
or	huòzhě	或者	conj	26
orange	júzi	橘子	n	19
orangeade, orange juice	júzishuǐ	橘子水	n	19
ought to	yīnggāi	應該	v-cog	26
outside	wàibiān	外邊	n	22**
outside	wàibiān	外邊	n	23
over	shàngbiān	上邊	n	22
overcoat, topcoat	dàyī	大衣	n	16**
painting	huàr	畫兒	n	26**
pair	shuāng	雙	measure	28
Palanka	Pàlánkǎ	帕蘭卡	prop	1*, 13*

English meaning	Pinyin	Characters	Functions	Lesson
paper	zhǐ	紙	n	5**, 13
park	gōngyuán	公園	n	28**
parlor	kètīng	客廳	n	22
particle, interrogative	ma	嗎	particle	2
particle, interrogative	ne	呢	particle	2
particle, modal	le	了	particle	13
particle, modal	a	啊	particle	17
particle, modal	ba	吧	particle	21
particle, modal	ne	呢	particle	2
particle, structural	de	得	particle	25
particle, structural	de	的	particle	5
particular	yídìng	一定	adj	20
pastry	diǎnxin	點心	n	24
peasant	nóngmín	農民	n	24
pen	bǐ	筆	n	5**, 13
pencil	bǐ	筆	n	5**, 13
people	rénmín	人民	n	26
person	rén	人	n	6
photograph	zhàopiàn	照片	n	21**, 23
pictorial	huàbào	畫報	n	11
picture	huàr	畫兒	n	26**
picture	zhàopiàn	照片	n	21**, 23
piece	zhāng	張	measure	16
plane	fēijī	飛機	n	29
please	qǐng	請	v-act	8
poem	shīgē	詩歌	n	26**
point	diǎn	點	measure	17
polite	kèqi	客氣	v-state	8
polite address to a lady	nǚshì	女士	n	9**
post office	yóujú	郵局	n	13**
present	lǐwù	禮物	n	21**

English meaning	Pinyin	Characters	Functions	Lesson
pretty	piàoliang	漂亮	adj	21
pretty good	búcuò	不錯	adj	25
professor	jiàoshòu	教授	n	13**
progress	jìnbù	進步	n	29
proverb	chéngyǔ	成語	n	26
pupil	xiǎoxuéshēng	小學生	n	27**
quarter (or an hour)	kè	刻	measure	17
question	wèntí	問題	n	18
quick	kuài	快	adj	25
reading room	yuèlǎnshì	閱覽室	n	15
real	zhēn	真	adj	21
reception	zhāodàihuì	招待會	n	27
red	hóng	紅	adj	19
referee	cáipàn	裁判	n	28
refreshments	diǎnxin	點心	n	24
representative	dàibiǎo	代表	n	23
request	qǐng	請	v-act	8
research	yánjiū	研究	n	26
right	yòubiān	右邊	n	22**
right away	jiù	就	adv	26
river	hé	河	n	25
road	lù	路	n	17
room	fángjiān	房間	n	22
ruler	chǐ	尺	n	5**
rural areas	nóngcūn	農村	n	24
sad	nánguò	難過	adj	29
scented tea	huāchá	花茶	n	19
schoolboy/girl	xiǎoxuéshēng	小學生	n	27**
schoolmate	tóngxué	同學	n	20
seat	zuòwèi	座位	n	16**
See you again	zàijiàn	再見	idiom	11

English meaning	Pinyin	Characters	Functions	Lesson
self	zìjǐ	自己	pron	30
serious	rènzhēn	認真	adj	24
set	tào	套	measure	22**
seven	qī	七	number	11
several	jǐ	幾	number	15
Shanghai	Shànghǎi	上海	n-prop	7*
she	tā	她	pron	5
ship	chuán	船	n	29**
shirt	chènshān	襯衫	n	16
shoes	xié	鞋	n	28
shop	shāngdiàn	商店	n	13
should	yīnggāi	應該	aux v	26
side	pángbiān	旁邊	n	22
sir	xiānsheng	先生	n	8**, 12
six	liù	六	number	11
skates	bīngxié	冰鞋	n	28
skating	huábīng	滑冰	v-comb	28
skating boots	bīngxié	冰鞋	n	28
skiing	huáxuě	滑雪	v-comb	28**
skirt	qúnzi	裙子	n	16
slow	màn	慢	adj	25
small	xiǎo	小	adj	22
smoke	yān	煙(烟)	n	8
snack	diǎnxin	點心	n	24
so	suǒyǐ	所以	conj	29
some	xiē	些	measure	24
sometimes	yǒu shíhou	有時候	idiom	18
son	érzi	兒子	n	21**
song	gēr	歌兒	n	19
soup	tāng	湯	n	25

English meaning	Pinyin	Characters	Functions	Lesson
South America	Nán Měi Zhōu	南美洲	n-prop	7**
spare time	kòngr	空兒	n	20
spoken language	kǒuyǔ	口語	n	15
sports	yùndòng	運動	n	28**
spouse	àiren	愛人	n	14
squad	bān	班	n	15**, 20
stadium	tǐyùchǎng	體育場	n	28**
staff	zhíyuán	職員	n	14**
stamp	yóupiào	郵票	n	13**
state	guó	國	n	6
still	hái	還	adv	15
story (of a building)	céng	層	measure	10
storied building	lóu	樓	n	27
student	xuésheng	生	n	9
studious	nǔlì	努力	adj	29
study	shūfáng	書房	n	22
sugar	táng	糖	n	19**
suitcase	xiāngzi	箱子	n	28
summer	xiàtiān	夏天	n	29
Sunday	xīngqīrì	星期日	n	20
supper	wǎnfàn	晚飯	n	26**
surely	yídìng	一定	adv	20
surname	xìng	姓	n	9
surname (, one's) is...	xìng	姓	v-id	9
sweets	táng	糖	n	19**
swimming	yóu yǒng	游泳	v-comb, n	25
switchboard	zǒngjī	總機	n	23**
table	zhuōzi	桌子	n	22
table tennis	pīngpāngqiú	乒乓球	n	28**
tea	chá	茶	n	8
teacher	lǎoshī	老師	n	6

English meaning	Pinyin	Characters	Functions	Lesson
team	duì	隊	n	28
telephone	diànhuà	電話	n	11**, 23
telephone call	diànhuà	電話	n	11**, 23
television	diànshì	電視	n	23
ten	shí	十	number	11
tennis	wǎngqiú	網球	n	28**
text	kèwén	課文	n	23
than	bǐ	比	prep	28
that	nà	那	pron	5
The Great Wall	Chángchéng	長城	n-prop	7*
The People's Daily	Rénmín Rìbào	人民日報	n-prop	23*
The Yangtze River	Cháng jiāng	長江	n-prop	7*
The Yellow River	Huáng Hé	黃河	n-prop	7*
the line is busy	zhàn xiàn	佔綫	idiom	23**
theatre	jùchǎng	劇場	n	16**
them	tāmen	他們	pron	3
them (for females)	tāmen	她們	pron	12
then	jiù	就	*conj	26
there	nàr	那兒	pron	10**
there	nàr	那兒	pron	15
there be	yǒu	有	v-poss.	14
therefore	suǒyǐ	所以	conj	29
they	tāmen	他們	pron	3
they (for females)	tāmen	她們	pron	12
thing	shì r	事兒	n	17
thing	dōngxi	東西	n	30
this	zhè	這	pron	4
this year	jīnnián	今年	n	20
three	sān	三	number	10
ticket	piào	票	n	16
tidy	zhěngqí	整齊	adj	25**

English meaning	Pinyin	Characters	Functions	Lesson
tight	jǐn	緊	adj	29
to	wèi	爲	prep	27
to	gěi	給	co-v	14
to act as	dāng	當	v-id	26
to act as a referee	cáipàn	裁判	v-act	28
to answer	huídá	回答	v-act	24
to answer (the phone)	jiē (diànhuà)	接(電話)	v-act	23
to arrive	dào	到	v-act	27
to ask	wèn	問	v-act	9
to ask	ràng	讓	v-act	19
to attend	bàn	辦	v-act	28
to attend	cānjiā	參加	v-act	20
to attend or to teach (a class)	shàng(kè)	上課	v-act	17
to be	shì	是	v-id	4
to be at	zài	在	v-loc	10
to be at ease	fàng xīn	放心	idiom	29
to be beautiful	piàoliang	漂亮	v-state	21
to be big	dà	大	v-state	16
to be black	hēi	黑	v-state	16**
to be blue	lán	藍	v-state	16**
to be busy	máng	忙	v-state	3
to be called	jiào	叫	v-id	9
to be called (or named) as	jiào	叫	v-id	9
to be conscientious	rènzhēn	認真	v-state	24
to be correct	duì	對	v-state	13
to be delighted	gāoxìng	高興	v-state	21
to be difficult	nán	難	v-state	24
to be excited	gāoxìng	高興	adj	21
to be few	shǎo	少	v-state	22
to be fond of	xǐhuan	喜歡	v-act	19
to be friendly	yǒuhǎo	友好	v-state	23

English meaning	Pinyin	Characters	Functions	Lesson
to be glad	gāoxìng	高興	v-state	21
to be going to	yào	要	v-int	19
to be going to	yào	要	adv	29
to be good	hǎo	好	v-state	1
to be good-looking	hǎokàn	好看	v-state	21
to be happy	gāoxìng	高興	adj	21
to be in	zài	在	v-loc	10
to be large	dà	大	v-state	16
to be like	xiàng	像	v-id	21
to be neat	gānjìng	乾净	v-state	21**
to be new	xīn	新	v-state	15
to be old	jiù	舊	v-state	16
to be polite	kèqi	客氣	v-state	8
to be pretty	piàoliang	漂亮	v-state	21
to be red	hóng	紅	v-state	19
to be right	duì	對	v-state	13
to be short of	chà	差	v-state	17
to be small	xiǎo	小	v-state	22
to be tidy	zhěngqí	整齊	v-state	25**
to be well	hǎo	好	v-state	1
to be white	bái	白	v-state	16
to be willing	yuànyì	願意	v-int	29
to be young	niánqīng	年輕	v-state	21
to beat	yíng	贏	v-act	28
to begin	kāishǐ	開始	v-act	27
to board	shàng	上	v-act	29
to borrow	jiè	借	v-act	15**
to buy	mǎi	買	v-act	13
to call (a taxi, etc.)	jiào	叫	v-act	29**
to call on	fǎngwèn	訪問	v-act	23
to call on (a person)	zhǎo	找	v-act	16

English meaning	Pinyin	Characters	Functions	Lesson
to chat	tán	談	v-act	20**, 26
to coach	fǔdǎo	輔導	v-act	20
to come	lái	來	v-act	13
to come in	jìn lái	進來	v-comb	26**
to come in	jìn	進	v-act	8
to come or go off work	xià bān	下班	idiom	17**
to come to a stop	tíng	停	v-act	25
to compare	bǐ	比	v-act	28
to compare	bǐjiào	比較	v-act	25**
to compete	sài	賽	v-act	28
to congratulate	zhùhè	祝賀	v-act	20
to cry	kū	哭	v-act	30
to dance	tiào wǔ	跳舞	v-comb	21
to deepen	jiāshēn	加深	v-act	26
to do	zuò	作	v-act	14
to do	bàn	辦	v-act	28
to do physical training	duànliàn	鍛煉	v-act	24
to draw	huà	畫	v-act	26**
to drink	hē	喝	v-act	8
to drive (a car)	kāi (chē)	開(車)	v-act	23
to eat	chī	吃	v-act	18
to enter	jìn lái	進來	v-comb	26**
to enter	jìn	進	v-act	8
to exercise	yùndòng	運動	v-act	28**
to fall ill	bìng	病	v-state	27**
to fish with a hook and bait	diào	釣	v-act	25
to follow	gēn	跟	v-act	17
to forget	wàng	忘	v-act	29
to get along	guò	過	v-act	30
to get into	shàng	上	v-act	29
to get married	jié hūn	結婚	v-comb	20**

English meaning	Pinyin	Characters	Functions	Lesson
to get on	shàng	上	v-act	29
to get someone angry/annoyed	qì én	氣人	idiom	28
to get up	qǐ chuáng	起床	idiom	18
to get up	qǐ	起	v-act	18
to give	sòng	送	v-act	21
to give	gěi	給	v-act	14
to give as a present	sòng	送	v-act	21
to go	qù	去	v-act	12
to go	zǒu	走	v-act	17
to go to bed	shuì jiào	睡覺	idiom	18
to go to work	shàng bān	上班	idiom	17**
to go to...	dào	到	v-act	27
to handle	bàn	辦	v-act	28
to have	yǒu	有	v-poss.	14
to have a pleasant journey	yílùpíng'ān	一路平安	idiom	29
to have fun with	wánr	玩兒	v-act	23
to help	bāng	幫	v-act	22
to help	bāngzhu	幫助	v-act	22
to hire (a taxi, etc.)	jiào	叫	v-act	29**
to interpret, to translate	fānyi	翻譯	v-act	26
to introduce	jièshào	介紹	v-act	13
to judge	cáipàn	裁判	v-act	28
to kick	tī	踢	v-act	28
to know	zhīdao	知道	v-cog	20
to know	rènshi	認識	v-cog	12
to know	liǎojiě	了解	v-cog	26
to know how to	huì	會	v-cog	26
to lack	chà	差	v-state	17
to laugh	xiào	笑	v-act	30
to learn	xué	學	v-act	9
to learn	xuéxí	學習	v-act	9

English meaning	Pinyin	Characters	Functions	Lesson
to leave	líkāi	離開	v-act	29
to lend	jiè	借	v-act	15**
to let	ràng	讓	v-act	19
to like	xǐhuan	喜歡	v-act	19
to listen	tīng	聽	v-act	19
to live	zhù	住	v-act	10
to live	guò	過	v-act	30
to look	kàn	看	v-act	7
to look for (a person)	zhǎo	找	v-act	16
to lose	shū	輸	v-act	28
to make (a telephone call)	dǎ (diànhuà)	打 (電話)	v-act	23
to make progress	jìnbù	進步	v-act	29
to make use of	yòng	用	v-act	11
to meet	jiàn	見	v-act	29
to meet (a person)	jiē (rén)	接 (人)	v-act	23
to meet (to see) each other	jiànmiàn	見面	v-comb	29
to miss	xiǎng	想	v-act	14
to open	kāi	開	v-act	21
to paint	huà	畫	v-act	26**
to part	fēnbié	分別	v-act	29
to pay a visit	cānguān	參觀	v-act	23
to pay attention to	zhùyì	注意	v-act	29
to play	wánr	玩兒	v-act	23
to practice	liànxí	練習	v-act	24
to prepare	zhǔnbèi	準備	v-act	25
to progress	jìnbù	進步	v-act	29
to propose a toast	gānbēi	乾杯	idiom	27
to put in order	zhěnglǐ	整理	v-act	22
to put on	chuān	穿	v-act	16
to reach	dào	到	v-act	27

English meaning	Pinyin	Characters	Functions	Lesson
to read	kàn	看	v-act	7
to read (aloud)	niàn	念	v-act	24
to recognize	rènshi	認識	v-cog	12
to reply	huídá	回答	v-act	24
to research	yánjiū	研究	v-act	26
to resemble	xiàng	像	v-id	21
to return	huán	還	v-act	11
to return	huí	回	v-act	17
to review	fùxí	復習	v-act	23
to rise	qǐ	起	v-act	18
to say	shuō	說	v-act	13
to see	jiàn	見	v-act	29
to see (someone) off	sòng (rén)	送 (人)	v(-comb)-act	30
to see someone off	sòngxíng	送行	v-act	29**
to serve as	dāng	當	v-id	26
to set off	chūfā	出發	v-act	23
to set one's mind at rest	fàng xīn	放心	idiom	29
to sing	chàng	唱	v-act	19
to sit	zuò	坐	v-act	10
to skate	huá bīng	滑冰	v-comb	28
to ski	huá xuě	滑雪	v-comb	28**
to sleep	shuì jiào	睡覺	idiom	18
to smile	xiào	笑	v-act	30
to smoke	xī yān	吸煙	v-act	8
to speak	shuō	說	v-act	13
to stand	zhàn	站	v-act	29
to start	kāishǐ	開始	v-act	27
to start out	chūfā	出發	v-act	23
to stop	tíng	停	v-act	25
to straighten up	zhěnglǐ	整理	v-act	22

English meaning	Pinyin	Characters	Functions	Lesson
to study	xué	學	v-act	9
to study	xuéxí	學習	v-act	9
to study (a subject)	niàn	念	v-act	24
to swim	yóu yǒng	游泳	v-comb, n	25
to take a bath	xǐ zǎo	洗澡	v-act	22
to take a picture	zhào xiàng	照像	v-comb	29
to take a rest	xiūxi	休息	v-act	18
to take a seat	zuò	坐	v-act	10
to take off	qǐfēi	起飛	v-act	29
to take part in	cānjiā	參加	v-act	20
to talk	tán	談	v-act	20**, 26
to taste	cháng	嘗	v-act	27
to teach	jiāo	教	v-act	15
to tell	gàosu	告訴	v-act	14
to thank	gǎnxiè	感謝	v-act	21
to thank	xièxie	謝謝	v-act	8
to think	xiǎng	想	v-act	14
to tour	lǚxíng	旅行	v-act	29**
to travel	lǚxíng	旅行	v-act	29**
to try	shì	試	v-act	27
to understand	dǒng	懂	v-cog	24
to understand	liǎojiě	了解	v-cog	26
to use	yòng	用	v-act	11
to visit	fǎngwèn	訪問	v-act	23
to visit	cānguān	參觀	v-act	23
to wait	děng	等	v-act	17
to walk	zǒu	走	v-act	17
to want	xiǎng	想	v-intention	14
to want	yào	要	v-act	19
to watch	kàn	看	v-act	7
to wear	chuān	穿	v-act	16

English meaning	Pinyin	Characters	Functions	Lesson
to weep	kū	哭	v	30
to welcome	huānyíng	歡迎	v-act	8
to win	yíng	贏	v-act	28
to wish	zhù	祝	v-act	21
to work	gōngzuò	工作	v	14
to work out	yùndòng	運動	v-act	28**
to write	xiě	寫	v-act	14
today	jīntiān	今天	n	20
together	yìqǐ	一起	adv	17
toilet	cèsuǒ	廁所	n	10**
tomorrow	míngtiān	明天	n	23
too	yě	也	adv	2
too	tài	太	adv	16
top	shàngbiān	上邊	n	22
train	huǒchē	火車	n	24
trainer	jiàoliàn	教練	n	25
translator	fānyì	翻譯	n	26
trousers	kùzi	褲子	n	16**
true	zhēn	真	adj	21
two	liǎ	倆	measure	26
two	èr	二	number	10
two	liǎng	兩	number	16
U.S.A.	Měiguó	美國	n-prop	6**
umbrella	yǔsǎn	雨傘	n	11**
umpire	cáipàn	裁判	n	28
(unit)	gè	個	measure	15
(unit)	jiàn	件	measure	16
(unit)	tiáo	條	measure	16
(unit)	zhī	枝	measure	19**
(unit)	bǎ	把	measure	22**
(unit, hat)	dǐng	頂	measure	28

English meaning	Pinyin	Characters	Functions	Lesson
(unit, person)	wèi	位	measure	25
(unit, vehicle)	liàng	輛	measure	21**
upper outer garment	shàngyī	上衣	n	16**
us	wǒmen	我們	pron	6
volleyball	páiqiú	排球	n	28**
vegetable	cài	菜	n	25**, 27
vehicle	qìchē	汽車	n	29**
very	fēicháng	非常	adv	21
very	hěn	很	adv	2
visa	qiānzhèng	簽證	n	28
volume	běn	本	measure	15
waiter	fúwùyuán	服務員	n	19
waitress	fúwùyuán	服務員	n	19
Wang	Wáng	王	n-prop	8*, 15*
Wang Shuwen	Wáng Shūwén	王書文	n-prop	24*
want	yào	要	v-int	19
watch	biǎo	錶	n	17**
water	shuǐ	水	n	19
way	lù	路	n	17
we	wǒmen	我們	pron	6
week	xīngqī	星期	n	20
well-known	yǒumíng	有名	adj	26
what	shénme	甚麼	pron	7
What's your (sur)name?	guì xìng	貴姓	idiom	9
where	nǎli	哪裏	idiom	25
where	nǎr	哪兒	pron	10
which	nǎ	哪	pron	6
white	bái	白	adj	16
who	shéi	誰	pron	6
wife	tàitai	太太	n	8**, 21
will	yào	要	adv	29

English meaning	Pinyin	Characters	Functions	Lesson
window	chuānghu	窗户	n	22**
wine	jiǔ	酒	n	27
winter	dōngtiān	冬天	n	28
with	hé	和	conj	13
with	gēn	跟	co-v	17
word	cí	詞	n	24
work	gōngzuò	工作	n	14
worker	gōngrén	工人	n	23
world	shìjiè	世界	n	7**
writer	zuòjiā	作家	n	26
year	nián	年	n	20
year (age)	suì	歲	measure	20
yesterday	zuótiān	昨天	n	28
you	nǐ	你	pron	1
you (pl.)	nǐmen	你們	pron	4
you (polite form of "nǐ")	nín	您	pron	8
young	niánqīng	年輕	adj	21
young lady	xiǎojie	小姐	n	9**, 19
younger brother	dìdi	弟弟	n	3
younger sister	mèimei	妹妹	n	14
zero	líng	零	number	10